HABITS OF THE MIND

Critical Thinking in the Classroom

Loren J. Thompson

University Press of America, Inc.
Lanham • New York • London

Copyright © 1995 by
University Press of America,® Inc.
4720 Boston Way
Lanham, Maryland 20706

3 Henrietta Street
London, WC2E 8LU England

Library of Congress Cataloging-in-Publication Data

Thompson, Loren J.
Habits of the mind : critical thinking in the classroom / Loren J.
Thompson.
p.   cm.
1. Critical thinking--Study and teaching--United States. 2. Thought
and thinking--Study and teaching--United States.   I. Title.
LB1590.3.T54   1995   370.15'24--dc20   95-9575   CIP

ISBN 0-7618-0022-0 (cloth: alk ppr.)
ISBN 0-7618-0017-4 (pbk: alk ppr.)

⊖™The paper used in this publication meets the minimum
requirements of American National Standard for Information
Sciences—Permanence of Paper for Printed Library Materials,
ANSI Z39.48—1984

To

Mary Anne

Contents

Preface

This book is meant to refocus the current educational reform movement, which came to the fore in the early 1980s, from an organizational fixation to the classroom. Obviously this is a giant undertaking; some may say an arrogant one. But the intent is neither arrogant, nor unrealistic. The book may not achieve what I hope, but at least I have said what I believe to be of major importance for American public education today.

Reforming American education is almost as old as the American concept of education for the public. It is advantageous to analyze the historic American concept of education for all from a variety of perspectives. One, of course, is how it is organized. This is not unimportant, but in every reform effort in American educational history, organization has received the lion's share of attention.

Over and over critics of current American public schooling indicate that if Horace Mann would return he would see educational practices that are little changed from when he was superintendent of the Massachusetts schools in the early part of the 19th century. Although this is likely an over-statement, the point is worth pondering. Some will argue that this ought to be the case. It is, they will say, preferable to the superficial pontificating they are convinced is now typical of America's public schools. Others, of course, want to maintain the status quo in the belief that schooling in the nation is at a higher level of effectiveness than at any time in the history of the nation.

I have not intended to be neutral. It is implausible, unrealistic, even impossible to return to the practices of another era, just as it is myopic to assume that education today is good enough. If we want learning to improve, then we *must* improve what happens in classrooms.

Never in the history of the nation's schools have we placed the emphasis on the *potential* of the students in the way that is advocated in*Habits of the Mind.* The pendulum has swung from perhaps an over-emphasis on rote memorization to a stress on "thinking" with, in the latter case, little widespread focus on how that end, however nebulously stated, is to be achieved.

If an effective and efficient effort is to be made to improve the quality of schooling, then the thrust must be grounded in sound evidence and argument, within the academic and practical capabilities of teachers and focused squarely on instructional practices. All students must be challenged to reason with precision, within the context of the subject matter that is taught. Such an approach can be a new beginning - true reform - and not another educational fad.

LJT
Colorado Springs, 1995

Acknowledgments

Few academic books are the product of a sole author. Authors need the feedback of colleagues and people with production skills as well as those who will ultimately be the consumers of the work. Surely this is true of the development of *Habits of the Mind.* During the last four years, involving numerous drafts, a number of people have helped hone and refine what I wanted to say, and how I wanted to say it. Mary Anne Thompson, wife, teacher and colleague, persevered in reading the early drafts Her insights and recommendations were precise and abundantly useful. Those students who have taken my course in which the text was the manuscript of this book, have assisted me in identifying and deleting extraneous materials, reorganization that makes the total argument more coherent and with examples with which teachers can readily identify. I want to specifically acknowledge the good will of Barbara Schmitt, a teacher in the Cheyenne Mountain School District in Colorado Springs, who granted me permission to excerpt her description of an activity she carried out with second grade students. And I owe a debt of gratitude to those individuals who read the manuscript and gave me valuable professional guidance: Brian McMahon of Colorado Springs, Diane Byrnes, a teacher in Arlington, Texas; Francis Kilkenny, a retired professor who now resides in Victoria, British Columbia; Colonel William McCabe, U. S. Army, retired, who carefully read the manuscript twice; Professor Gerald Reagan, The Ohio State University; Bonnie Stewart, a teacher in Arlington, Texas; Ann Thompson, President of the University Learning Center, Pierre, South Dakota; and Colonel Mal Wakin, chairman of the philosophy department at the United States Air Force Academy. Finally, I wish to acknowledge the assistance of Tom Spiers of the University of Colorado at Colorado Springs who graciously did the tedious computer work. I, however, am responsible for whatever weaknesses yet remain in the book.

Introduction

We are what we repeatedly do. Excellence, then, is not an act but a habit.

Aristotle

It is [education's] business to ingrain into the individuals working habits, methods of inquiry and reasoning. The formation of these habits is the Training of Mind.

John Dewey

Today's dissatisfaction with public education did not suddenly burst onto today's scene. Abigail Hamilton, a late 19th century Boston writer, opined the state of education in Massachusetts in the 1890s:

> The school system of Massachusetts, with all its supervision and all its superintendence, and all its expensiveness, is so ineffective, it so magnifies and nourishes itself, and so neglects, not to say dwarfs, the pupils, that a child may go through the whole course from the primary to high school inclusive without a single absence or tardiness and receive his diploma of graduation, and come out thoroughly illiterate, absolutely under-educated, absolutely untrained - with no accomplishment except slang, with no taste above dime novels, with neither brain nor nerve nor muscle braced for the battle of life....The taxes of the people go to fatten 'organization' and the children suffer.

Mrs. Hamilton's lament sounds remarkedly, regretably current. Given the striking similarities between what she describes and what modern schooling has become, it is amazing we have not learned thatsimply restructuring bureaucracy, if basic changes in teaching and learning are neglected, will lead to few if any appreciable improvementsin learning. Habits of clear, precision reasoning must be an integral part of all teaching and learning.

Habits are important. An early 19th century French visitor to the

United States, Alexis de Tocqueville, commented on the "habits of the heart" of the American people. Late in the 19th century, into the 20th, William James, then John Dewey, counseled teachers that life is a "mass of habits," and that education "consists in the formation of wideawake, careful, thorough habits of thinking."

From the beginning of the American Republic to well into the 19th century, the public school curriculum was essentially classical in content, designed for the privileged. In the early years of the 20th century, progressive thinkers in education, following the lead of political progressives, set out to change that focus. The pendulum shifted in the direction of making the curriculum more practical, the means of instruction more diverse, and the opportunities for an education more widespread. Later critics charged that liberal teaching methodologies have been mistaken for "liberal education." They are not entirely wrong.

This book is about learning reasoning skills as subject matter is learned, but in the broader sense it's about the total strengthening of education in America. It's about rigorous thinking, simplicity, setting priorities, sorting out values and solving problems. It argues that the skills of logic and analysis, which develop the habits of clear and precise thinking, will markedly strengthen the education of students. Overtly and implicitly, the book argues that the illogical tension between the learning of subject matter and the mastery of reasoning skills should be set aside.

The book is written to be used in teacher education, both at the graduate and undergraduate levels, and for in-service education courses for practicing teachers. It will fill a long-standing need for professors of the philosophy of education. *Habits of the Mind* demonstrates the *use* of logic. There is no intention either to turn teachers into logicians or for them to teach students logic as an academic discipline. The writing is deliberately straightforward, neither "textbookish" nor glib. And the book does not cover all of the needs of education. For example, the many questions and responses raised by psychology are not part of the discussion. A model for incorporating reasoning skills into the teaching and learning of subject matter is proposed in chapter 1 and carried throughout the book.

If America's public schools are to be reformed and if reform indicates improvement, then at least five crucial concerns must drive the reform of public schools. First, the focus must be on the classroom. Early inthe 1980s, Carolyn D. Wyatt, in a symposium address she calls, "...a missing and essential element...," counseled: "There will continue to be bureaucratic efforts to mandate and to dictate strategies for the improvement of schooling. But real improvement must come from the school itself, and even more specifically, from instruction in the classroom." In the same symposium, the Massachusetts Commissioner of Education said, "The heart of educational reform is in what goes on in the classroom, not in how performance is measured. *Higher standards are the result of reform, not the cause.*" [Italics added.]

Second, complacency must be overcome. Both common sense and historical precedent indicate the foolishness of "throwing out the baby with the bath water." Reform is not simply to mollify the critics. Substantive changes that will result in the teaching process and the skills of teachers rising to new heights must be made.

Third, public educators, with the cooperation and understanding of the general public, must delimit what they attempt to accomplish. At some point both educators and Everyman must be impressed with the reality that it is misguided, probably impossible, to expect schools to cope effectively with all of society's problems.

Fourth, quality must be viewed as a continuum, not as a fixed point. Everyone wants "quality" education. But for what level of quality are we willing to settle? To assume that higher standards, without the requisite means of achieving the standards, amount to "quality education," is at best fuzzy thinking. Gerald Reagan of The Ohio State University argues that traditional academic freedom has promoted "freedom from" and it is now time to promote "freedom to." "Freedom to" can lead us to move out of the quagmires of intellectual conflicts which cause us to see education as a series of bifurcations: either we emphasize this or that, never stopping to consider that both this and that may be desirable and possible. For most of the nation's history, an impressive array of writers have stepped to the plate to take a swing at what is wrong. It is time to stop the bashing and "get on with it." "Freedom to" will not happen unless the means to such an end are identified, mastered and utilized.

Fifth, educators at every level must understand and be able to use the techniques of both inductive and deductive reasoning, and in practice be able to marry the two. Such a marriage has been called for by scientists, philosophers and educators. Aristotle recognized the functions and importance of induction, but preferred deduction. Francis Bacon favored the use of induction, but likely would be surprised thatAmerican educators have given up so completely on the use of deduction. Induction is the most sophisticated reasoning conceived by man. It is the process used to generate knowledge. But inductive conclusions are always probable, never absolute; they are always subject to change. On the other hand, deductive reasoning, which Bertrand Russell asserts has never produced one bit of knowledge, is a useful analytical tool. The conclusions that result from inductive reasoning become the knowledge learned in schools. Given the tentative nature of all knowledge, students need to know how to examine what they are expected to learn, that is the conclusions reached by the reasoning of someone else. As Fustel de Coulanges says, "Years of analysis are required for one day of synthesis."

Within the last century, academicians such as John Dewey, William James and Jerome Bruner have wrestled with how to make schools into places where serious, systematic reasoning is an integral part of the curriculum; where the atmosphere exudes strong, serious, focused thinking. Within the last generation, educators such as Robert Ennis, B. O. Smith, Ronald Munson, Thomas Green, and historians Michael Katz, Diane Ravitch and Lawrence Cremin, to mention a few, have suggested programs in logic and analysis for teachers. This book turns their suggestions into an action plan.

It's not sufficient simply to assert that schools have gone to hell in a handbasket. The world has changed dramatically and teaching and learning have not. Will and Ariel Durant, have conjectured that "if the transmission [of civilization]" - a classic function of education - "should be interrupted for one century, civilization would die, and we should be savages again." To fail to clearly delineate the twin needs to learn subject matter and to do so with precision thinking is to take a step toward interrupting the transmission of civilization.

There is a compelling need to reinstate intellectual excitement in schools, to cast aside such archaic and destructive notions that only a small percentage of students can learn academic material. In a critique of the reports on education which appeared in the 1980s, A. Harry Passow says, "What seems to be missing from many reports is a meaningful discussion of the intrinsic worth of education - the pleasure of learning..." In the abstract, Passow is correct. But to assume that the pleasure of learning can be separated from the formation of intellectual habits would be misguided. It's time to integrate reasoning skills into subject matter, ground the learning of reasoning skills in the works of intellectual masters and package the programs so they are usable by teachers. It's time to employ a vocabulary that is common to all educators and to the historic reasoning vocabulary that is our heritage.

For decades we have mouthed the rhetoric that in schools, students "learn to think." Of course they do. They can think before they arrive at school. But whether or not they can *reason* creatively and with precision, and get excited about doing so, is another question. Reality needs to match rhetoric.

A former United States Commissioner of Education, Harold Howe II, prods us to remember that the ineloquent response to which educators all too often resort is neither necessary nor sufficient to deal with the imperatives of modern educational reform. "When in trouble or in doubt, run in circles, yell and shout," is Howe's characterization of the modern educator's response to criticism. Mindless despair, absent the requisite knowledge and skills, will not upgrade quality.

The quantity of critical thinking that is taught and learned in classrooms must increase; this is necessary if education is to challenge and fulfill the potential of the millions of students whose futures are held captive by the education they now receive. But the quantity of critical thinking that is taught is not sufficient to meet the standards that America and America's schools must reach. *High* quality must have its day. *Habits of the Mind* addresses this imperative.

In chapter 1, a distinction is made between thinking and thought. Some assumptions on which American education has long been premised are also examined and two primary goals for the simultaneous teaching of subject matter and reasoning skills are proposed. The chapter ends with some hypotheses about strengthening teaching and learning.

Truth and knowledge and the claims human beings make to know truth are discussed in chapter 2. Conditional reasoning is the focus of chapter 3. How to turn statements into propositions then into arguments is examined.

Some of the strengths of class reasoning as a teaching tool are examined in chapter 4. Chapter 5 expands the discussion with specific emphasis on conditional reasoning as a teaching tool.

Chapters 6 and 7 are about language in the reasoning and teaching processes. Definitions, metaphors and slogans are given specific attention.

Informal fallacies, those mistakes in reasoning and in the use of language which are outside the framework of formal reasoning, are the focus of chapter 8.

xiii   Chapter 9 examines and demonstrates how the skills of critical thinking can be used to solve problems.

Chapter 10 succinctly synthesizes the major thrusts of the book. A different paradigm from the ones currently in use, one that combines the teaching of reasoning and the mastery of subject matter for all students at all levels, is offerred.

The final chapter is followed by references, appendices and an index.

Chapter 1

A Context For Knowing

The only safeguard against reasoning ill is the habit of reasoning well; familiarity with the principles of correct reasoning, and practice in applying those principles.

John Stuart Mill

Reason is the self-discipline of the orginative element in history. Apart from the operations of Reason, this element is anarchic.

Alfred North Whitehead

In *Posterior Analytics,* Aristotle states what has proven to be the lasting value of deductive reasoning: to demonstrate truth. *Habits of the Mind: Critical Thinking in the Classroom,* focuses on the use of deductive reasoning skills, primarily from Aristotle, and the contributions of the philosophical analysts, within the last two centuries, to make the case that a new pedagogy is needed in America's schools. The chapter begins with a discussion of the differences between thinking and thought. Then four assumptions that have long affected American education are reviewed and some essential reasons for incorporating reasoning skills into the learning of subject matter are identified and defined. The chapter concludes with four hypotheses which, if taken seriously, can improve the dysfunctional aspects of the teaching paradigms presently used. The chapter and the entire book suggest a context for teaching and learning that fuses subject matter and reasoning skills into a single paradigm. This paradigm is summarized in chapter 10.

Thinking and Thought

Early in the 20th century, John Dewey separated thinking, as a process, from thought, as the end result of the process. From Aristotle to Heidegger, the same distinction has been made.

In American schools more attention is given to teaching thought than is given to teaching thinking. Often neither are adequately learned. There is no compelling mandate that the acquisition of information should be emphasized at the expense of reasoning skills. The needs of students to think with clarity and precision as they learn subject matter simply have not been appropriately addressed. There is a definite place for both subject matter and memorization, *but the memorization of academic information comes nowhere near being the sum of an education.*

Students need control over intellectual skills as well as over information to enable them to examine the information. The lack of integration of the skills of reasoning into the learning of subject matter is based on some long-standing assumptions in American education that are at best questionable.

Assumptions And Their Functions

All teaching and learning are based on assumptions. Without making assumptions it would be impossible to either teach or operate schools Assumptions reflect points of view, what is already believed to be true. Lawrence Thomas puts the reality of making assumptions into perspective when he says, "There is no view without a point of view." When, however, assumptions are left unstated or unrecognized the result may be fuzzy practice and distorted learning. Dewey warns, "that when a wrong theory once gets general acceptance, men will expend ingenuity of thought in buttressing it with additional errors rather than surrender it and start in a new direction." While the importance of every assumption is not the same, there are some assumptions embedded in American educational planning and practice that should be examined as a prerequisite to any consideration of the reconstruction of American education.

Four Assumptions In American Education

For many years, regardless of how manifested, the following

assumptions have been implicit but largely unexamined planks in the American educational platform:

Assumption #1: Students must build up a sizable reservoir of subject matter information *before* serious, analytical thinking can begin.

Assumption #2: The process of acquiring information sharpens the mind for serious thinking *about* subject matter.

Assumption #3: Memorization of information makes a positive difference in the overt reasoning behaviors of people.

Assumption #4: Teachers can effectively teach reasoning skills even though *they* have not learned precise reasoning processes.

None of the assumptions are either totally untrue or totally misguided. But individually and collectively, the ways in which they are applied causes them to have an unfortunate effect on the achievement of American students. All four assumptions have been too little examined while being too widely followed.

Assumption #1 is largely a myth. Symbolic logic and mathematics are subject matter examples that explode the assumption. So does the ability of soldiers and others to react instantaneously and appropriately when confronted with totally new, sometimes life-threatening situations. The myth is further eroded when young children spontaneously raise incisive questions about what they observe and hear.

The learning of information is obviously important. But the assumption in question has led both educators and non-educators to accept a linear model for learning that requires a predetermined level of information before the processes of reasoning can be energized. We can think without reasoning, but we cannot reason without thinking. Thinking is the weaker of the two terms. To reason in depth and with precision, information is indeed needed. Lest we be victimized by Goethe's admonition that "Knowledge tricks us beyond measure," we should be acutely aware that everyone, including the very young student, is constantly thinking.

Assumption #2 also assumes a linear model for learning. And it too is largely a myth. Human beings probably do create individual "models of learning" in their minds in attempts to deal effectively with what they are expected to learn. But to presume that the mind functions exactly the way a taxonomy looks is too restrictive, too simplistic and eventually dysfunctional.

The human mind *may* learn in a serial way, but the processes of learning manifest themselves differently in different individuals. To assume that the mind must be "sharpened" with knowledge before it can begin the process of analytical thinking is not a supportable hypothesis. Alfred North Whitehead, early in the 20th century, frames the point clearly and unequivocally: "I have no hesitation in denouncing it [the assumption in question] as one of the most fatal, erroneous, and dangerous conceptions ever introduced into the theory of education. The mind is never passive; it is a perpetual activity, delicate, receptive, responsible to stimulus. You cannot postpone its life until you have sharpened it."

Assumption #3 rests on the dubious hypothesis that the memorization of information will increase reasoning powers, influence value choices and make a positive difference in individual preferences and decisions. There is little or no evidence to support such an assumption. Unless education goes *beyond* the intake of information, students have not learned all that is needed to enable them to function productively in a complex world. Nietzsche is provocative, if not prophetic, when he says, "Many a man has failed to get a proper education because his memory was too good."

There is an irony here. In some schools, memorization of literature such as great documents and poetry has been ignored, even debunked. But deemphasizing memorization has not been replaced with the practice of having students learn precise, sound reasoning skills. Memorizing is a worthwhile and necessary educational practice, but memorization is simply not sufficient to claim that a student is educated. In Charles Dicken's *Hard Times,* students in Mr. Gradgrind's school could memorize the bones of an animal but did not understand that the bones outlined a horse. In too many places education has moved little beyond Mr. Gradgrind's model. In Whitehead's words, students need "to learn the art of the utilization of knowledge."

Assumption #4 may be the most seductive of all. It is the "better caught than taught" contention. Most American teachers were educated in American schools which have either explicitly or implicitly embraced the first three assumptions. But rarely have teachers been taught the logical processes and techniques of how to use knowledge and intellectual skills to enhance learning.

Students are frequently left to their own devices to figure out how to reason. At best, they are left to pick up indirect cues. The degree to which such a practice persists varies. Sometimes reasoning processes are learned in one curriculum area - truth tables are taught in mathematics, for example - but are neither developed fully and systematically nor carried across the curriculum. Denis Doyle characterizes the current practice of paying too little attention to the need of all students to reason with clarity and precision as "startling." This book focuses on two reasons for the direct teaching of the skills of logic and analysis, as subject matter is taught and learned. These reasons are carried throughout the text.

Two Reasons for Teaching Reasoning Skills With Subject Matter

1. To develop clear, precise thinking skills. The concept of precision thinking has been high on the list of educational priorities throughout the course of Western history. For example, in the High Middle Ages, Peter Abelard challenged his contemporaries by asserting that doubt leads to inquiry and inquiry leads to truth. Research, examination and reasoning, all of which can result from intelligent doubt, are important stepping stones in the quest for truth. Whitehead places this notion in the same perspective in which we are placing it here: "In the process of learning there should be present in some sense or other, a subordinate activity of application. In fact, *the applications are part of the knowledge.* For the very meaning of things known is wrapped up in their relationship beyond themselves. Thus unapplied knowledge is knowledge shorn of meaning." "All genuine education," Dewey said, "terminates in discipline, but it proceeds by engaging the mind in activities worth while for their own sake." These activities are "genuine education" because they have meaning when they are examined using reasoning skills.

Sometimes it is difficult to find what information means in a world overburdened by verbal and written communications. Classroom presentations, books, classroom discussions, explanations and other instructional activities may lack clarity for some students because the reasoning employed is imprecise and the language used is unclear. In the early 1920s, two British professors, C. K. Ogden and I. A. Richards, in *The Meaning of Meaning,* argued eloquently for the imperative to never stop short of meaning as a learning goal. Only by assuring that students have the capabilities to reason clearly and precisely can we be confident they will at once get from and give back to life the fullest measure of which they are capable.

The lad who returns home from doing yard work in the neighborhood and tells his father that he earned $10 and 50 cents and 35 cents needs to think with more precision and more clarity. Both ends can be achieved when he learns that if you add the 50 cents and the 35 cents to the $10, then the total is $10.85. Another example makes the same essential point. To tell students that Caesar crossed the Rubicon may be neither precise nor clear. But to teach them to reason that 1) if Caesar is to return to Rome by land, then he must cross the Rubicon, and 2) if he crosses the Rubicon, then the likely results will be... leads to precision thinking and the clarification of how and why this event occurred, the results of which changed Western history.

2. *To understand the nature of the knowledge.* Understanding the nature of knowledge is a concern that is introduced into formal education far too late. The academic disciplines each have their own "nature".

Aristotle says, "the kind of reasoning demanded in any subject must be such as the subject matter itself allows." In similar fashion, Professor Thomas Green argues, "the teacher must know the methodology of his subject and the limitations of its findings....the teacher must have a feeling for logic, proof, and evidence." Subject matter does, indeed, keep education alive, but epistemology should have a great deal to do with how subject matter is taught, and epistemology demands that we know something of the nature of the subject matter.

Every academic discipline has a structure or nature that in important ways is unique to that discipline. There is no reason to assume that we either can or need to discover a generic structure of knowledge that will "fit" every discipline. Questions need to be raised such as, What is unique about history? about mathematics? about biology? about physics? How do all of these bodies of knowledge differ and how are they alike? How is each area of knowledge used? To understand how the nature of knowledge and the relationships of diverse bodies of knowledge can enhance both the acquisition of subject matter and our capabilities to reason are involved in this critical point.

Some Theory and a Model for Knowing

To paraphrase former presidential cabinet member, John Gardner, unless educators become precise and thorough about teaching students reasoning skills as subject matter is taught, from plumbing to physics, neither our theories nor our pipes will hold water. Theory is a systematic way of guiding and accounting for practice. Theory grows out of what is already known and enables us to connect what we know and understand with new ideas that have yet to be confirmed. For example, when Dr. Walter Reed observed what was happening in Panama in the 19th century he connected what he learned - such as the presence of large numbers of mosquitoes - with an hypothesis that the mosquitoes might be causing the disease of yellow fever. He created a theory to connect what was known with what was believed but not known. The terror of yellow fever was successfully confronted.

To make systematic progress in any endeavor, including educating, the informed use of theory is important. Theory is not wild speculation;

it is a plan for proceeding. Theory enables us to determine our direction, to organize our efforts, to set priorities, to understand the adversities to be overcome, to have confidence in our work. Scholars have long pointed out that theory provides us with the tools to describe, explain and predict outcomes in every field of work, including educating.

Models are used to make theory understandable and useful. Typically, a model is used either as a copy of what we want to achieve, or the ideal of what we want to do, or as the standard against which we measure whether or not what we set out to do was accomplished; in practice, conceptual models of theory can achieve all three. For instance, when a teacher wants students to write properly, she may have them copy and follow a well-written paragraph. She teaches how to write a proper paragraph then evaluates their writing against the model paragraph. In this case, the theory is that students can structure well-written sentences and paragraphs, using the language skills they have learned earlier, to follow the writing of someone else. The model paragraph serves as a copy, an ideal and a standard for evaluation. The theory is reflected in the model.

Education does not suffer from a lack of conceptual models. Unfortunately, the models currently dominant in U. S. schools, which have been used for well over half a century, have been imposed upon the American public by default; a more effective model has not been offered and used. To address this need, the core arguments in this book are premised on four pivotal hypotheses.

1. The assumptions inherited from the past must be examined and either discarded or modified if they cannot be supported by evidence and sound reasoning.

2. Students will have the intellectual prerequisites to embark on a lifetime of learning when specific, proven reasoning skills are incorporated into the teaching and learning of ssubject matter.

3. Students will have a continuing framework within which learning can be couched when they acquire the skills to reason clearly and precisely and to understand the nature of the subject matter in which they are being tutored.

4. Teachers cannot sufficiently incorporate the skills of reasoning into subject matter until they have mastered the skills themselves.

Direct teaching is neither necessary nor sufficient to becoming an educated person. Nevertheless, we should not and likely will not stop teaching. But if students are to acquire the dispositions and skills to become life-long learners, then teaching must become more efficient and more effective, while at the same time becoming less obtrusive.

This book demonstrates how subject matter can be taught at any level so that students master the skills of careful reasoning and at the same time understand the information and the nature of the subject matter being learned. In the process, the often unexamined assumptions upon which current educational practice is too frequently premised will be clarified and the mastery of the subject matter itself will be enhanced.

Chapter 2 is an examination of truth and knowledge, then an explication of how to recognize and use truth claims.

Applications

1. In this chapter, two reasons are given for using reasoning skills to teach and learn subject matter. Which of the two reasons is best represented by each of the following statements?

   a. George Washington either cut down a cherry tree or he didn't.
   b. "Now it's Istanbul, not Constantinople..."
   c. Two plus two equals four and Benedict Arnold aided the British.
   d. Most children enjoy stories.

2. In the following statements, identify which of the four assumptions which have long guided much of American education corresponds to each statement.

   a. It's stupid to expect first graders to think; they first must learn.
   b. If you want students to become responsible for their own lives, have them memorize information.
   c. Once the Table of Elements is memorized, students will be able to solve chemical equations with unswerving accuracy.
   d. It doesn't matter that he has had no formal education in reasoning, Mr. Knowel can teach students everything they need to know; he is a certified teacher.

See Appendix B for responses.

Chapter 2

Truth, Knowledge And Truth Claims

Give me the liberty to know, to utter, and to argue freely according to conscience, above all liberties.

John Milton

...for thought is the highest of our activities, as reason is the highest of our faculties, and the objects with which reason is concerned are the highest that can be known.

Aristotle

All men possess by nature the desire to know.

Aristotle

Greek intellectuals, particularly the philosophers of the Golden Age, represent an historic step forward in man's ancient quest to know truth. Alfred North Whitehead brings into focus the contributions of the great Greek thinkers: "The real importance of the Greeks for the progress of the world is that they discovered the almost incredible secret that speculative Reason [*sic*] was itself subject to orderly method." In this chapter, we briefly explore the concepts of truth and knowledge, and how human beings can claim to know truth. Understanding such distinctions is basic to an "orderly method of reasoning."

Truth

According to the late Richard Hofstadter, "the pursuit of truth is said to be at the heart of the intellectual business..." Likewise, Plato wrestles with the distinction between truth and falsity in an attempt to define knowledge. From Aristotle to Aquinas to the present, human beings have pursued truth. But what is truth? Is truth evidence, as John Dewey said or the conformity of an idea to its object as Martin Heidegger said? In the New Testament record, Christ says to his followers, "You shall know the truth and the truth shall make you free." Then at the trial of Christ, the Roman officer Pilate asks, "What is truth? In the *Meno*, Socrates addresses the distinction between knowledge and truth in a straightforward, bold-sounding statement: "That there is a difference between right opinion and knowledge is not at all a conjecture with me but something I would particularly assert that I know. There are not many things of which I would say that, but this one, at any rate, I will include among those that I know."

Although what we know is not restricted to what is "directly evident," Philosopher, A. J. Ayer, has said, unequivocally, that the man who knows, as opposed to the man who only has an opinion, is the man who has a "right to be sure." By equating "know" with "has a right to be sure," Ayer is saying that when we claim to know we have evidence. To state a fact is to state truth; to deny a fact is to deny truth. Being able to support a claim to know truth is important. On this point, the philosopher T. V. Smith once said, "Only that man knows, who knows how he knows, and can so exhibit this technique that others may know how he knows, or may know, by the same token, that he does not know."

As used in this book, "truth" rests on either 1) evidence that supports a claim to know, 2) the logic used to reach the conclusion or 3) a claim to know that cannot be supported by either evidence or logic, but is still part of the reality of life as human beings perceive and live it. The first claim to know truth - based on the evidence we have to support the claim - we will call a "synthetic" claim. The second - which we deem to be true because of the language of the logic used to express the claim - we will call an "analytic" claim. And the third - which we may hold to with great tenacity, but which can be supported neither by evidence nor logic - we will call "metaphysical". These three ways of claiming to know truth are discussed later in the chapter.

But first, we need to be clear about what is knowledge and what is truth. The differences between knowledge and truth are captured in the contention that if it is not true we cannot claim to know it. A proposition can be true and not be known; it cannot be known without being true.

Knowledge

Knowledge is inextricably linked to truth, but is not the same as truth. Truth is reality, which can be known to the extent that a person is willing to apply himself to the task of learning. To know is to grasp at least part of what is true. In the 17th century, the French philosopher, Rene Descartes, concluded that mind and matter operate "parallel" to each other. By taking this position he avoided direct confrontation with the church over the question of whether or not mind and reality are separate. Many modern thinkers contend that Descartes' explanation did not succeed. Gilbert Ryle, a British philosopher, refers to Descartes' explanation as "the myth of the Ghost in the machine". In the world of philosophy, Descartes' efforts are often referred to as the "Cartesian Compromise," reflecting his understandable reluctance to confront directly the power of the church which taught that truth, and therefore knowledge of truth, is absolute, not relative.

First, it is possible to know *if and only if* something occurred. For example, to claim to know what was said in the Magna Carta would be nonsense if no such document had been written. It is not possible to know something that is not the case. Second, the would-be knower must believe that what is claimed to be known did in fact occur. If we are to know that Magna Carta was agreed to at Runymede in 1215, it is necessary to believe that the document was written and agreed to at that place and time. To say that we know this information, but do not believe it would be nonsense. Third, to know - in the strongest sense - we must have evidence. In summary, we can claim to know Q *if and only if*

Q occurred;
we believe Q occurred; and
we have evidence that Q occurred.

As we will see, however, the claim to know can also be grounded in either logic or metaphysics. But before reaching that point, another distinction is important. When we claim to know, regardless of the grounding in which the claim is rooted, we are at the same time asserting that we either *know how* or *know that*, or both.

Knowing That

The distinction between knowing *how* and knowing *that* is a stellar contribution to modern thinking. Having control over either information or ideas is *knowing that*. For instance, to know that the morning sun appears first in the eastern sky is to *know that*. And to know who was Secretary of State when the People's Republic of China established diplomatic relations with the United States is to *know that*. That *all* the information about Q is not available to us does not vacate a claim to know Q. If the requirement is that *all* must be known, such a requirement says that we can never know. In some cases, for example, all the evidence is simply not available. Information has to be synthesized and compared with other information that may bear on Q, then inferences have to be made. Inferences - commonly called conclusions - are what we know when we *know that*. It is possible to *know that* even when we do not have direct access to *that*. If this is not the case, then claims to know in such areas as history and many of the sciences are vacuous claims.

But to *know that* about any specific matter does not necessarily mean that *knowing that* will never change. When what was known at one point is shown to no longer be true, because either the evidence or the interpretation of the evidence changes, then what was formerly *known* can no longer be known. For example, scientific *knowing* was for many years based on Newtonian physics. The knowledge generated using Newtonian hypotheses and laws propelled scientific knowledge forward with amazing speed, when compared to the pace of scientific learning in all earlier times. But the work of Albert Einstein in the 20th century has blunted much of what was *known* through Newtonian science. The paradigm for viewing and analyzing the universe changed based on new methods of experimentation and different ways of interpreting and using data. Now scientists know different from what Newtonian scientists knew; however, it would be inaccurate to say that these earlier scientists did not know. On the other hand, when we ask "Do they know it and can they do it?" we are asking two separate but related questions: "Do they *know that* ? and do they *know how?*"

Knowing How

In the mid-20th century, Gilbert Ryle gave life and vigor to the distinction between the concepts of mind and body. Ryle wrestled with a distinction that had bothered scholars, in general, since Thomas Aquinas, in the Middle Ages, and specifically Rene Descartes, in the 17th century. If *knowing that* means to have control over information or ideas, *knowing how* is to be able to *do* something, either physically or intellectually, Ryle reasons. We learn to *know how*, he says, by practice, not by theorizing (although we may learn *how* to theorize by theorizing).

Ryle makes a distinction between the terms *drill* and *training* that helps us understand his distinctions between knowing how and knowing that. He uses the word *drill* to identify the means of achieving habits and *training* to develop what he calls *"intelligent capacities,"* which we are grouping into the category called *knowing how*. We may say that after learning *that*, we must be able to use *that*, which is *knowing how*. "Habits of the mind," as the expression is used in this book, are acquired through what Ryle labels training, rather than by simple rote drill. Using this distinction, drill is a part of training but training is not a part of drill. Either drill or training, or both, may be *necessary* to know how, but alone neither is *sufficient* to know how. Knowing how is understanding as well as having the skills to either physically or intellectually manipulate objects and ideas.

Knowing how is procedural knowledge. Ryle says, "Overt intelligent performances are not clues to the workings of minds; *"they are those workings"* (emphasis added). A quarterback knows how to grip and throw a football; a professor knows how to lead students to think conditionally; the senate majority leader knows how to get legislation through the red tape of congress, Jose knows how to get a yes from his father when he believes his mother would undoubtedly say no. Knowing how is being able to either physically or intellectually use knowledge. And because we can claim to *know that* and *know how* in more than one way, we need to clearly understand and be able to use the various ways in which it is possible to claim to *know* truth.

Claims to Know Truth

The authority in which we ground a claim to know truth is different from the methodology used to acquire the knowledge. A claim to know because of the logic of the language used to make the claim is called an *analytic* claim; a claim to know that requires evidence to support it is called a *synthetic* claim; and a claim to know that does not meet the criteria of either logic or evidence is called a *metaphysical* claim.

Analytic Claims

A claim to know is analytic when the subject and predicate of a statement mean the same thing. Logician Roderick Chisholm says, "It might be suggested that the truths of logic and other truths of reason stand in this peculiar relationship to language: they are true solely in virtue of the rules of our language or solely in virtue of the ways in which we use words." Such claims are called "analytic" because it is possible to know truth without accumulating evidence. We can know by analyzing the language used to make the claim itself.

Aristotle recognizes that a claim to know, based on evidence, is different from a claim to know that is not based on evidence. A claim not supported by evidence he refers to as "opinion." Both Leibnitz, in the 17th century, and Kant, in the 18th, recognize two different ways of knowing. Many modern philosophers, such as John Stuart Mill and John Dewey, also acknowledge the distinction between analytic and synthetic claims. Philosopher and educator Thomas Green, who believes in analytic claims, says: "...an analytic statement is one whose truth or falsity can be ascertained by a mere inspection of its logical form or by examining the meaning of the words used to express the statement." The most conservative philosophers, however, assert that "a boundary between analytical and synthetic statements simply has not been drawn." This contention is explicated more fully in the section in this chapter on synthetic truth claims.

Analytic statements need no proof external to the statement itself. There is simply no need to investigate to see if every bachelor or every spinster is unmarried. The use of the words has already indicated the absence of a spouse. And proponents of analytic claims point out that a statement such as "a circle has 360 degrees," is obviously analytic because the subject and predicate have the same meaning. Outside of a complete redefinition of how the universe operates, including a recasting of the number of degrees in a circle, there is nowhere to go when the question of whether or not a circle has 360 degrees is raised; when the word "circle" is heard, everyone understands 360 degrees.

We sometimes "make" a word analytic to achieve an end far removed from the normal use of the word itself. Retired Colonel Harry A. Summers reflects on this point in an article in *Foreign Affairs*: "For many years nuclear weapons were such an important part of our national military strategy that they virtually defined the word *strategic*, which classically had meant the use or threatened use of military means to achieve the political ends of the state. At the beginning of the nuclear age, in a brilliant semantic maneuver, the nuclear theorists hijacked the word and misappropriated it to advance their conviction that nuclear bombs were 'strategic' weapons capable by themselves of achieving the political goals and objectives of the United States. As a result, for many years *strategic* almost automatically meant the use of nuclear means, as in the phrases *strategic forces, strategic weapons,* and *Strategic Air Command* ." This example also demonstrates that the use of language sometimes brings about a change in thinking, which is not an unimportant consideration.

Analytic claims are necessary to teaching and learning. When we say "sugar" we do not have to add "is sweet" for fear of not being understood. Without analytic statements we would be compelled to say every word, such as, "Sugar is sweet" or "Fire is hot" or "An ophthalmologist is an eye doctor". But if we assume that the general understanding of the use of a subject term obviates the need to add the redundant predicate, the statement is no less analytic. Robert Frost's observation that "Poetry is the kind of thing poets write," is analytic; so is, "My father is my male parent."

Immanuel Kant, who gave us the term *analytic,* stipulates three necessary criteria for a statement to be analytic:

1) the predicate is contained in the subject;
2) the connection between the subject and predicate is one of identity; and
3) if we can deny either the subject or predicate we are involved in a self-contradiction.

The rejection of analytic statements is sometimes based on practical grounds that have little or nothing to do with usage. For example, logician W. V. Quine sums up his objection to analytic claims by saying that philosophers already make too many distinctions. The assertion appears to deny the utilitarian link between language and learning. But such an assertion does not go unchallenged. Philosophers Grice and Strawson maintain, "On the whole, it seems that philosophers are prone to make too few distinctions....It is their assimilations, rather than their distinctions, which tend to be spurious."

To escape the use of analytic claims would be difficult, if not impossible. To recognize them and intelligently strive to assure that students recognize them is basic to clear thinking and satisfying communications. For example, one reviewer reports that a fourth grade state history textbook contains the statement, "A natural boundary is a boundary that exists in nature." The claim is, of course, true. And it is analytic. If a teacher does not recognize this point, how will the students be affected? Would a teacher assign students to research such a claim? Such would be a nonsense assignment; claims subject to research are synthetic claims.

Synthetic Claims

"Synthetic" is used to indicate that verification of a claim comes from empirical evidence, outside the claim itself. Perhaps more than anyone else, those thinkers who demand evidence to support a claim to know are indebted to the work of the 18th century Scottish philosopher, David Hume. Hume divides reasoning into two categories, that which he calls "demonstrative reasoning...and that concerning matters of fact and existence." As his life and career progressed, Hume tilted heavily in the direction of matters of fact. A strong leaning in the direction of verification by evidence can also be seen in the works of such 20th century philosophers as John Dewey and William James. For instance, Dewey says that "making sure" means garnering evidence. The end of such an inquiry, he says, is the attainment of "knowledge or truth." To equate knowledge and truth with evidence is the bedrock on which synthetic claims rest. An uncomplicated example of a synthetic claim can be seen in a statement from an introductory textbook:

> For some periods, as between 1936-1939, and 1949-53, it is insufficient to describe the U. S. S. R. as totalitarian - it was in fact what could be called a terror-society, where no citizen, regardless of his position or the degree of loyalty to the regime could feel safe.

The claims to know in this statement can be *believed* as a result of the language used to express them, but they cannot be verified by simply analyzing the language. Evidence of mass murders and widespread purging directed by Josef Stalin can, however, be gathered to support the claim of a "terror-society."

Modern empiricists reject the claim that knowing can be grounded in anything other than evidence. One such scholar, A. J. Ayer resolutely asserts, "The theist, like the moralist, may believe that his experiences are cognitive experiences, but unless he can formulate his knowledge in propositions that are empirically verifiable, we may be sure that he is deceiving himself." Early in the 20th century, the eminent psychologist, William James takes virtually the same position when he says, "True ideas are those that we can assimilate, validate, corroborate and verify. False ideas are those that we cannot."

Although modern empircists reject Kant's reasoning about analytic claims, they accept his criteria with which a synthetic claim must be consistent:

1. The predicate lies outside the subject.
2. The connection between the subject and predicate is not one of identity.
3. Synthetic claims can be denied without self-contradiction.

An excerpt from Alan Moorehead's *The Russian Revolution*, illustrates Kant's criteria:

> During 1906 and 1907 violence became almost part of daily life in Russia: it is estimated that in these years alone some four thousand people were murdered.

First, the predicate in Moorehead's statement - an estimate of the number of people murdered in Russia in 1906 and 1907 - is outside the subject: "violence became almost part of daily life in Russia." Even though murder is indeed violence, the murders could have occurred at one calamitous, horrific time rather than having been distributed as "almost part of daily life." Second, the connection between the subject and predicate is not one of identity. They are complementary statements, but either statement can stand alone. Violence could have been manifested in a variety of ways. Third, either the subject or the predicate can be denied without denying the other.

Although it is not uncommon for someone to make an analytic claim when intending to make a claim that is synthetic, synthetic claims are made constantly without either the evidence or the source of the evidence being revealed. An example from an American autobiography, *Land of the Burnt Thigh*, a story of hardship and commitment in early 20th century South Dakota, illustrates the ubiquitous use of synthetic claims. Edith Eudora Ammons Kohl, who with her younger sister homesteaded in the Dakota territories, relates that in 1909 she received a letter from a St. Louis investor, Halbert Donovan, in which he made the following statements:

> We are beginning to feel the effect of a business expansion back here which the western land development seems to be bringing about. If it continues, with all the public domain that is there, it is bound to create an enormous demand in industry and commerce.

Implicit in his statements are several synthetic claims: A revival in business is the direct result of western land development, and continued development can bring about a great demand in commerce and industry. Even though Mr. Donovan offers no empirical evidence to support his claims, they are both couched in cause and effect relationships and can either be verified or denied.

But some claims can be supported neither by evidence nor by reasoning; nevertheless, such claims may be a significant part of everyday life. We use the term *metaphysical* to identify such claims.

Metaphysical Claims

Metaphysical claims to know truth can be supported neither by evidence nor the logic of the language used to express them. The British philosopher, Thomas Hobbes (1588-1679), refers to metaphysics as "first philosophy": Human beings experience life before being able to explain it. We also know that long before people were able to either logically or empirically account for much of the phenomena in life, they accounted for what they did not understand by the invention of myths as a means of explanation.

The term, "metaphysical" comes from the combination of two Greek words: *meta,* which is used to indicate "before," or "prior to," or "after the physical" and *physical,* indicating the tangible realities of the world in which we live. In general usage, metaphysics, since ancient times, has been considered to be the study of the ultimate nature of reality and the universe. As used here, the term refers to that part of life for which there is neither a logical nor an empirical verification.

Simply to label claims that cannot be supported either by logic or by evidence as "sophistry and illusion," as Hume asserts, does not provide a framework for dealing with the totality of life as human beings are capable of experiencing it. There is a need for a mechanism to nurture understanding, not one to hasten rejection.

As used here, the concept of the metaphysical in everyday life becomes clear when we examine specific instances. Writing in *Foreign Affairs,* Robert W. Tucker and David C. Hendrickson explain the practical reasons for President Thomas Jefferson's reluctance to allow the United States to become involved in a war at the beginning of the 19th century. According to the authors, in Jefferson's view a war "would introduce into the republic all the elements of its corruption - debt, taxes, standing armies, artificial privileges of all kinds, ultimately an enlargement of executive power that would lead to the reintroduction of monarchy." Tucker and Hendrickson then conclude, "This was Jefferson's deepest instinct, and though he drew close to war on many occasions throughout his life and indeed sometimes wished clearly that war might come to purge his rage against foreign transgression, in the end he nearly always drew back." How does a student separate the various kinds of truth claims made by the authors? The synthetic claims are not a difficult problem. But we can effectively deal with the authors' assertions about Jefferson's instincts and what he "wished clearly" only if we are willing to acknowledge and accept the claims as metaphysical. We can verify what Jefferson said and did (because evidence has been left) but we cannot convincingly verify what were his "instincts."

When the French philosopher, Rene Descartes, was faced with the need to explain the existence of God, he resorted to a complicated formula: 1) Everything, including ideas, has a cause; 2) we have an idea of God; 3) nothing short of God is adequate to cause our idea of God; therefore, 4) God exists. But can this explanation weather close analysis? For example, what is the justification for asserting that everything has a cause? And since God has not been seen, how is it possible for human beings to conceive of him? In what is the claim grounded that nothing short of God can cause the idea of God? Reduced to its basic meaning, Descartes' claim says, "Nothing short of God can cause the thought of God." But another approach is educationally more appropriate. It is more educative and more credible to account for such phenomena by teaching students systematic ways to confront the metaphysical than it is to either eschew the concept or attempt to force it into what may be an inappropriate category. To do so weakens neither analytic nor synthetic claims.

We have mentioned myths. So what about myths? From Aesop to the present, human beings have indulged in, been entertained by, studied and profited from myths. Myths have long been used in an attempt to explain the unknown. Can the content of myths be accounted for either logically or empirically? Their effects may be, but not the myths themselves. In this book, we take the same position assumed by journalist Thomas Friedman: "Myths are primarily what give people the faith to undertake projects which rational calculation or common sense would reject." Myths are part of our heritage and should be dealt with, in the context of education, in a reasoned way. In the absence of either evidence or supportive logic, myths are metaphysical claims to know.

Life continues to reflect what the physicist Michael Polanyi calls the "tacit dimension". There are aspects of life that defy empirical assessment, but they are still part of reality. In the face of criticism that a metaphysical statement is "neither a tautology nor an empirical hypothesis" or that it is an *ersatz* statement, "outside the realm of real statements," current and future generations will continue to be confronted with the need to deal with the metaphysical.

The young deserve to learn that the openness of Protagoras, in his 4th century B. C. play, *On the Gods*, is a desirable trait. Today giant strides have been made to deal with the metaphysical realities that both delighted and confused the ancient author:

As to the gods, I have no means of knowing that they exist or that they do not exist. For many are the obstacles that impede knowledge, both the obscurity of the question and the shortness of human life.

Applications

1. Explain the kinds of truth claims being made in each of the following statements.

a. Human beings can live for long periods without water.
b. A spinster has a husband.
c. A god will give me the answers to these questions.
d. The states are all over the map on this.
e. Whenever government spending grows faster than the econmy, the deficit rises.
f. This square has four sides.
g. Susan thinks Bill is handsome.
h. $2 + 2 = 4$.
i. High above the heavens God created.

2. Identify each of the following statements as eithera claim to *know that* or a claim to *know how*. Some claims may be both:

a. Fuel, oxygen and an igniter are necessary to have fire.
b. $2 + 2 = 4$.
c. I understand the formula.
d. I can solve the problem.

e. Ophelia is in love.
f. His stance looks awkward, but he can throw the football with great accuracy.
g. To go to the moon is more than a day's walk.
h. Tonight I'm going to repair my VCR.
i. You have to be able to recognize an argument and relate the premises so that the argument is valid.
j. Sean recited the poem without a single mistake.

See Appendix B for responses.

Chapter 3

Conditional Reasoning

According to our evidence the first logicians to debate the nature of conditional statements were Diordorous Cronus and his pupil Philo.

William & Martha Kneale

We may state that all reasoning, without exception, is built around the structure of conditional statements.

Thomas Green

Although the roots of conditional reasoning predate the intellectual heyday of Greece, it is in the modern world that "if, then" reasoning has become widely utilized. But there has been no widespread effort in elementary and secondary education to infuse these skills into the teaching and learning of subject matter. This chapter examines the basic concepts of conditional reasoning and the promise these skills have for teaching and learning. Socrates sets the stage.

Some Lessons From Socrates

In one of Plato's minor dialogues, Socrates provides some examples of conditional ("if, then") reasoning, a keen insight into the epistemological position held by some 4th century B. C. Athenians and the importance of both recitation and analytical - sometimes popularly called "Socratic" - questioning. In the following excerpts from Plato's *Meno*, Socrates is involved in a series of discussions with Meno and

Meno's servant boy. Some analysis of the conversation follows the excerpt. Since the dialogue is lengthy, those parts of the conversation between Socrates and the slave boy which involve only the clarification of geometric dimensions are omitted.

[Socrates has Meno summon a servant boy who speaks Greek. The questioning and reasoning processes then begin.]

Socrates:	Tell me, boy, do you know that a figure like this is a square?
Boy:	I do.
Socrates:	And you know that a square figure has these four lines equal?
Boy:	Certainly.
Socrates:	And these lines which I have drawn through the middle of the square are also equal?
Boy:	Yes.
Socrates:	A square may be of any size?
Socrates:	Do you observe, Meno, that I am not teaching the boy anything, but only asking him questions; and now he fancies that he knows how long a line is necessary in order to produce a figure of eight square feet; does he not...?
Socrates:	Now see him being brought step by step to recollect in regular order. (To the boy.) Tell me, boy, do you assert that a double space comes from a double? Remember that I am not speaking of an oblong, but of a figure equal every way, and twice the size of this - that is to say of eight feet; and I want to know whether you still say that a double square comes from a double line...? *[The dialogue continues.]*
Socrates:	What do you say of him, Meno? Were not all these answers given out of his own head?
Socrates:	And at present these notions have just been stirred up in him, as in a dream; but if he were frequently asked the same questions, in different forms, he would know as accurately as anyone at last?
Meno:	I dare say.
Socrates:	And this spontaneous recovery of knowledge in him is recollection?
Socrates:	And this knowledge which he now has must he not either have acquired at some time, or else possessed always?

Socrates:	And if there are always to be true notions in him, both while he is and while he is not a man, which only need to be awakened into knowledge by putting questions to him, his soul must remain always possessed of this knowledge; for he must always either be or not be a man.

Socrates utilizes three distinct questioning techniques. First he uses *recitation questioning*, questioning that probes for information. For example, such questions as, "do you know that this figure is a square?" is seeking information. Socrates has disdain for "learning" that is not defined as recollection. He strongly suggests that the servant boy already "knows" from his experiences in a prior life. Socrates is concerned that this epistemological point be clear to Meno. To reinforce his position, Socrates asks Meno such questions as "Does he learn from me or only remember?" and "does he really consider?" Modern educators are able to demonstrate empirically that students learn information, either through their own experiences or by being directly taught. Although today's educators have a different view of the nature and genesis of knowledge from what Socrates and Plato held, the questioning technique to determine whether or not a student remembers is essentially unchanged.

Socrates' second technique is *analytical questioning*. Meno's attention is immediately and pointedly focused on the moment when the servant boy "fell into perplexity under the idea that he did not know and had a desire to know." Meno is obliged to respond to Socrates' questions, such as, "But still he had interests in those notions of his had he not?" Meno acknowledges that it seems the boy is not taught information, but rather recalls it.

Socrates' questioning also demonstrates that it is virtually impossible to have a reasoned discussion without at the same time bearing on the concept of epistemology. When he asks the servant boy "do you know that a figure is a square?" he deals with knowledge, whatever the source. But when he follows by asking, "And you know that a square figure has these four lines equal?" he goes beyond the knowledge level; when we know that a figure like this is a square, then we know that a square figure has four lines equal. Socrates is probing to determine if the knowledge has meaning for the boy.

His third questioning technique is designed to lead the learner to a *synthesis*. Socrates is in fact inquiring into the learner's ability to see relationships and move to a level where what has been learned can be summarized in a conclusion. The knowledge is not simply stored in the learner's memory, but he can *use* the knowledge.

Without distorting Socrates' meaning, his questioning can be converted to conditional ("If, then") statements: "If he learns from me, then..." and "If he only remembers, then..." When either students or teachers complete the "then" part of the statement, a conditional statement is created. But more importantly, a statement is developed that mandates further inquiry, research and reasoning.

Either directly or by implication, conditional reasoning utilizes the format of "if, then." A ditty, repeated for generations, illustrates the concept of conditional reasoning:

If ifs and buts are candy and nuts, then every day is Christmas.
Ifs and buts are candy and nuts.
>Every day is Christmas.

Even though the argument is nonsense, it is correctly formed. The premises are properly related and the conclusion is necessary - there can be no other conclusion. Whether or not it is true that every day is Christmas is an empirical question, subject to verification. As a widely used form of deductive reasoning, conditional reasoning *demonstrates* truth - or what can be demonstrated as *not* being truth.

Sentence Reasoning

Sentence reasoning begins with a complete statement. Conditional reasoning is a form of sentence reasoning and depends on a statement that is framed in an "if, then" context. In those areas where symbols other than words are the tools of the trade, the term "sentence" is also often used; for example, we speak of a mathematical "sentence," meaning a mathematical statement in which a complete thought is expressed. To learn to think with clarity, precision and understanding we need to examine the components of sentence reasoning, beginning with the concept of a sentence.

Sentences

Communication is carried on principally through language, therefore in sentences. Not infrequently, however, what is *said* is not the literal message the sender intends to convey. For example, a statement that may appear to be a declarative sentence that gives information - "I certainly enjoyed the day with you" - may be nothing more than a ceremonial statement of politeness. The message is graciousness, not "let's do it again, soon." And it is also the case that the distinctions between the kinds of sentences learned for grammatical purposes, and the uses of sentences in reasoning, are not necessarily the same. Grammatically correct sentences are important, but do not necessarily convey crisp reasoning simply because they are grammatically accurate. Every complete English sentence has at least one subject and one predicate. To a large extent, the study of grammar is the study of whether or not the relationships between the subject and predicate are proper. In reasoning, the techniques of logic are used to examine similar relationships, but for the purpose of improving clear, precise understanding. For instance, "If Erick swings the bat, then he will hit the ball" is a complete, compound sentence. The nouns and predicates in both parts of the sentence are relatively easy to spot: "Erick swings" and "he will hit." In reasoning, the sentence can be divided into the antecedent (the "if" part) and the consequent (the "then" part). The truth of the antecedent is conditional to the truth of the consequent: *If* Erick swings the bat, *then* he will hit the ball.

Propositions

A statement (sentence) that either explicitly or by implication can be shown to be true or false, right or wrong, that can either be believed or disbelieved, is a proposition. Since the latter half of the 19th century, philosophers in the Western world have focused heavily on the analysis of propositions. It is by means of propositions that most thinking is expressed. The expression used to refer to such reasoning is *propositional logic.*

The examination of language as a conveyor of thought presumes that *use* determines the meaning of a word. The use of the term *proposition* is an example. Another word, such as *statement*, could be used. In the literature of reasoning, however, including most textbooks, the word *proposition* is used. Although within the context of reasoning the terms *proposition* and *statement* are often used in much the same way, the two terms are not exact synonyms. *Statement* is a broader term than *proposition*. Many kinds of statements are not propositions. Propositions are different from questions, exclamations, requests or commands, all of which are statements and may be spoken or written as sentences. A question may be asked, an exclamation uttered, a command given; however, none of these can be either affirmed or denied or proven to be true or false.

Often only careful examination of a statement will unmask its intended message. To use the techniques of conditional reasoning to examine a statement, we need first to change the statement into a proposition - a declarative statement. But before we change a statement to a proposition, we need to understand some other characteristics of propositions.

Every proposition has both *quality* and *quantity*. The quality of a proposition refers to whether it can be affirmed or denied, and whether it is positive or negative. The quantity of a proposition refers to whether it is *universal* ("all" or "none") or *specific* ("some"). A proposition can be either universal or specific, positive or negative. Therefore, four kinds of propositions can be stated:

Universal and Positive: All school board members are properly motivated.

Universal and Negative: No school board members are properly motivated.

Specific and Positive: Some school board members are properly motivated.

Specific and Negative: Some school board members are not properly motivated.

When we assert that "all" of a group meet a certain criterion, or standard, there is no room for deviation. The same is the case when we use "none." These are absolute expressions. And to assert that either all or none of a group are properly or improperly motivated is judgmental. "Some" is qualitatively less absolute, but also makes a distinction. "Universal" is quantitative. "Positive" and "negative" are qualitative. Once a sentence is stated as a proposition, however, it can be turned into a conditional statement.

Conditional Statements

Whether stated directly or by implication, conditional reasoning is always either couched in or presumes an "if, then" format. In some contexts, "if, then" reasoning is referred to as "cause and effect" or "means-consequent," or "didactic," or "hypothetical" reasoning. But whatever it is called, this form of thinking is conditional reasoning. If one part of the statement is true, the *condition for its truth* is the truth of the other part of the statement.

Not every conditional statement is a causal argument. P does not always cause Q. Sometimes "if, then" statements are nothing more than explanations of what has occurred and serve the same function as any other declarative sentence. When "if, then" reasoning is used to establish causality ("If it is raining, then there are rain clouds") conditional reasoning is being used in such a way that a logical argument can be formulated. But when "if, then" reasoning is used simply to account for something ("In this climate, if it gets cloudy then it is almost certain to rain") an explanation, not an argument, is being made.

As noted in the discussion of sentences, a conditional statement asserts that the first part of the statement, the antecedent, implies the second part of the statement, the consequent. The antecedent is the part of the statement which begins with *if* and the consequent is the part which begins with *then*. No claim is made that the antecedent is true, only that *if* it is true then its truth is sufficient for the consequent to be true; and the truth of the consequent is necessary to the truth of the antecedent. (The concepts of necessary and sufficient are examined later in this chapter.)

When a teacher says, "Take out your math books and turn to the chapter on fractions, beginning on page 55," she makes a statement that is a command. To analyze the statement, we can treat it as proposition, then turn it into a conditional statement:

> If you take out your math books and turn to page 55, then we can start our study of fractions.

The conditional statement can now be turned into a *conditional argument*.

Conditional Arguments

An old French proverb says, "It is from the clash of opinions that the truth spurts out." Although experience tells us that clashing opinions do not always yield truth, the proverb demonstrates that the term *argument* is widely thought of as disagreement. At some point almost everyone disagrees with someone else. But there is a crucial distinction between *argument*, as often used in everyday discourse, and *logical argument*. In everyday disagreements, the "arguments" that ensue do not always lead to either truth, clear thinking, valid reasoning or satisfying solutions to problems. Such disagreements may be highly seasoned with emotion and result in clouding rather than clarifying issues.   On the other hand, a logical argument strips away the emotional contexts in which propositions are sometimes couched and shows the true relationship of one proposition to another. Lord Chesterton put the concept of logical argument into clear focus when he said, "Generally, people quarrel because they cannot argue." Thomas Green sums up the synonymity between argument and logic when he says, "logic is the study of argument."

Conditional arguments are built on four basic rules of inference, all of which are used repeatedly in everyday life. The first rule of inference is *Modus Ponens* , meaning, *to affirm the antecedent*. Modus Ponens says that if P occurs, then Q will result:

Modus: If Sean exceeds the speed limit, then he may get a traffic ticket.
Ponens: <u>Sean exceed the speed limit.</u>
         >Sean gets a traffic ticket.

When we affirm the antecedent we restate the "if" part of the sentence as a second premise. In effect, the restatement says that the antecedent as stated in the first premise is true and only one conclusion can be reached.

A second rule of inference, the converse of Modus Ponens, is *Modus Tollens*, to deny *the consequent:*

Modus: If Sean exceeds the speed limit, then he may get a traffic ticket.
Tollens: <u>Sean does not get a traffic ticket.</u>
         >Sean does not exceed the speed limit.

In Modus Tollens the second premise denies the consequent in the first premise, therefore the antecedent, which relies on the truth of the consequent, is also untrue. *Modus Ponens and Modus Tollens* are the two most basic rules of conditional reasoning. But two other rules are not infrequently used.

The third rule of inference is the *disjunctive rule* , the "either, or" rule: *either P or Q,* but not both. In the case of Lisa, the message is "either, or":

Disjunctive All students must either study the assignment or they will
Rule: not learn the material.
             <u>Lisa is a student and she studies the assignment.</u>
             >Lisa learns the material.

These arguments are equal to saying, "*Either* students study the assignment *or* they will not learn the material." Whether argued Modus Ponens or Modus Tollens, the conclusion is the same: Students have a choice, to study and learn, or not to study and not learn, but they cannot have it both ways.

In making decisions, students must learn not to narrow the focus too narrowly too quickly. In any situation, all alternatives need to be recognized and considered. Then they can identify the most reasonable alternative. Sometimes "either, or" situations are not recognized; on other occasions, situations are seen as "either, or" when in fact there are other alternatives. (Caution should be exercised to avoid the fallacy of bifurcation, which is discussed in chapter 8.)

The fourth rule of inference is the *conjunctive rule,* the rule that includes *both* P and Q. The language can be either direct or implied.

Anna avoids legal difficulties by living in accordance with the laws which emanates from the Constitution and enjoys the privileges guaranteed by the Constitution.

When couched in a conditional format, the statement says

Conjunctive Rule:	If Anna both lives by the laws which emanate from the Constitution and avoids legal difficulties, then she will enjoy the privileges guaranteed by the Constitution.

The use of all deductive reasoning, including conditional reasoning, is to make explicit the content of the premises. When in the first premise two statements are combined into a proposition and arranged into an "if, then" format, a proposition has been converted to a conditional statement. When the conditional statement is properly combined with a second premise (and a conclusion necessarily follows) a conditional argument is made.

If students take out their math books and turn to page 55, the study of fractions can begin.
Students take out their math books and turn to page 55.
>They can now begin the study of fractions.

Another example, using a statement from the media, allows us to see a conditional argument embedded in reasoning about serious matters of the world. Reporting on a wire service story about the differences between the quality of the World War II materiel of the Americans and the Germans, one author points out that by 1945 the German armed forces had equipment superior to that of the Americans. The question historians and other analysts ask is, What if the Germans had had superior equipment as early as 1940? At least two propositions are embedded in this consideration: 1) By 1945 the Germans had military equipment superior to the U. S. and 2) Superior equipment could have made a difference in the outcome of the war had it been available to the Germans as early as 1940. These propositions can be changed to a conditional statement without changing their meanings:

If the high quality of military equipment available to the Germans in 1945 had been available 1940, then the outcome of World War II may have been altered.

By adding a second premise, argued either Modus Ponens or Modus Tollens, and reaching a conclusion, an argument is created:

If the high quality of military equipment available to Germany in 1945 had been available in 1940, the outcome of World War II could have been altered.
The outcome of World War II was not altered.
>The Germans did not have as high quality military equipment available in 1940 as in 1945.

Whether or not the conclusion is true depends upon the truth of the premises. In this case, truth can be determined by empirical research.

After an argument is made it can and should be tested to determine if it is sound. A sound argument is valid and the premises are true. *The test for validity should always precede the test for truth.*

Truth and Validity

Every conditional argument has at least two premises and a a conclusion. To the premises two defining terms are attributed: *truth and validity.* Truth is the property of propositions, or statements. Premises are propositions. Premises can be proven to be either true or false, depending on the evidence or the logic of the language used to express them. Validity is the property of arguments. When two premises are stated, and only one conclusion can necessarily follow from the premises, a valid argument has been formed. In everyday discourse it is not uncommon to hear people use the terms truth and validity as if they are synonymous. In the language of reasoning, they are not. In logic, truth and validity have two distinct uses, therefore two distinct meanings. Logic is concerned primarily with validity. Truth presumes validity. Our ability to know more and more truth is directly related to the precision and accuracy of our reasoning. An example illustrates the concepts of truth and validity:

If Soviet Communist leaders have long been noted as tough negotiators, and Josef Stalin was a Soviet Communist leader, then he was a tough negotiator.
Soviet Communist leaders have long been noted as tough negotiators and Josef Stalin was a Communist leader.
>Josef Stalin was a tough negotiator.

The argument is sound because it is both valid and true. It is valid because as the premises are stated, only one conclusion necessarily follows. The premises are true because they can be supported with evidence.

To be able to recognize a valid from an invalid argument is critical. There are two basic forms of invalid argument that sometimes masquerade in the mantle of validity, but which are in fact mistakes.

These mistakes are the reverse of the valid forms of argument we have examined earlier and are referred to as *logical* or *formal fallacies*. One invalid form is the *fallacy of affirming the consequent* ; the other is the *fallacy of denying the antecedent*. The fallacy of *affirming the consequent* is seen in the following argument:

> If Lauren has a dog, then his name is Snoopy.
> His name is Snoopy.
>
> \>

At first glance, it may appear that "I have a dog" is the proper conclusion. But the argument is invalid. While the argument form is deceptively like a valid form, such an arrangement of premises can only lead to an improper conclusion and to imprecise reasoning. The same argument can be used to illustrate the fallacy of *denying the antecedent*:

> If Lauren has a dog, then his name is Snoopy.
> Lauren does not have a dog.
>
> \>

No necessary conclusion can be reached. If the truth of the consequent is conditional, based on the truth of the antecedent, then denial of the antecedent invalidates the consequent and there is no argument. It can't be both ways. To know how to form arguments that are both valid and true is essential to sound reasoning. Even then, however, arguments can and should be tested further.

We have referred to premises being necessary and sufficient. Sometimes arguments that appear to be solid and compelling are, upon examination, found to be unsound. An unsound argument is an argument that either has an invalid form, untrue premises, or both. In the following section, we look at the concepts of necessary and sufficient and the biconditional as ways to test conditional arguments further.

Necessary and Sufficient

A. J. Ayer, a British academic logician, says, "one can understand a sentence perfectly well, and yet be puzzled when it comes to giving an account of the conditions which are necessary and sufficient for the truth of the proposition which it expresses." The rule to determine whether or not a conditional statement meets the necessary and sufficient conditions is straightforward: *In a conditional statement, the truth of the antecedent is a sufficient condition for the truth of the consequent, and the truth of the consequent is a necessary condition for the truth of the antecedent.* A *sufficient* condition for the occurrence of an event is a circumstance in whose presence the event must occur. A *necessary* condition for the occurrence of an event is a circumstance in whose absence the event cannot occur. An example illustrates the two concepts:

> If we plant a bean in soil where it gets light, oxygen and water, then it will sprout.
> We plant a bean in soil where it gets light, oxygen and water.
> >The bean will sprout.

Planting a bean in soil where it gets light, oxygen and water are sufficient conditions for the bean to sprout. But it is not necessary that the bean be planted in soil, have light, oxygen and water for it to sprout. The bean may not sprout for a variety of reasons other than not being planted and nourished properly. Or it may be planted in a substance other than soil. In this case the truth of the consequent is not *necessary* to guarantee the truth of the antecedent.

On the other hand, sometimes arguments are stated so that both the rules of necessary and sufficient apply:

> If Lauren expects to pass freshman English, then she must demonstrate an understanding of *Hamlet*.

Passing freshman English is *sufficient* evidence to conclude that a student has demonstrated an understanding of *Hamlet*. And demonstrating an understanding of Hamlet is also *necessary* to pass freshman English. Absent evidence that a student understands *Hamlet*, receiving a passing grade in the course will not happen. Use of the concepts of necessary and sufficient guarantees that the most compelling conclusion possible has been reached. Such an argument is a biconditional.

The Biconditional

When both the concepts of necessary and sufficient apply, a conditional statement can be stated as a *biconditional*. A biconditional is stated in the language of "if and only if". A biconditional requires that a statement not simply be either necessary *or* sufficient, but that it be both. A student can expect to pass freshman English, *if and only if* she is able to demonstrate an understanding of *Hamlet*. The concepts and their usefulness can be outlined by first setting up a conditional statement:

> Lauren will be given credit for freshman English *if and only if* the she manifests an understanding of *Hamlet*.

The statement can be transformed into the following biconditional argument:

> If and only if he demonstrates an understanding of *Hamlet*, will Lauren be given credit for freshman English.
> Lauren manifests an understanding of *Hamlet.*
> >Lauren is given credit for freshman English.

So far, the discussion of conditional reasoning has centered on reason ably simple statements and single arguments with two premises. In reality, much reasoning is frequently more complicated. Often students and teachers must deal with a chain of reasoning.

Chains of Reasoning

Sentence reasoning quite frequently consists of multiple premises, linked in ways that may make it difficult to determine whether or not the conclusion follows from the premises. John Locke called chain reasoning "Demonstration knowledge" indicating that as the chain lengthens increasing clarity should result. When an argument with multiple premises is encountered use can be made of some relatively simple techniques to determine if an extended series of propositions are related in a logical way and the conclusion necessarily follows. The process is a more involved use of simple conditional reasoning. The following short example illustrates the concept of chain reasoning:

> To know what something is is to know what it is *for*; to know what something is for, we must learn what is its nature, its character, its *form*.

The author spins out an argument with multiple premises. The statements are linked together and lead to a single conclusion. Since the statement is already a series of propositions, it can easily be changed into several conditional statements:

> If we claim to know something, then we must know what it is for.

> If we know what something is for, then we must know what is its nature, its character, its form.

> If we know its nature, its character, its form, then we know what it is for.

> If we know what something is for, then we can claim to know it.

A second premise can be added to each conditional statement and then a conclusion can be reached. Adding a second premise and reaching a conclusion for every statement that is included in the chain may not be necessary, but for purposes of clarity and understanding, these steps are taken in the following chain:

1.0 If we claim to know something, then we must know what   it is for.
1.1 We claim to know something.
1.2 >We must know what it is for.

2.0 If we know what something is for, then we must know what is its nature, its character, its form.
2.1 We know what something is for.
2.2 >We know its nature, its character, its form.

3.0 If we know its nature, its character, its form, then we know what it is for.
3.1 We know its nature, its character, its form.
3.2 >We know what it is for.

4.0 If we know what something is for, then we know it.
4.1 We know what it is for.
4.2 >We know it.

The last conclusion leads back to the original claim, which in this case is the first conditional statement.

To follow a chain of reasoning, begin with the conclusion, which quite often is the initial premise in the chain, and follow it through. Sometimes the reasoning may be written in a convoluted way so that the premises are not in the order in which the reasoning actually flows. This problem can be corrected by rearranging the premises so that the reasoning can be followed in an orderly sequence. The following paragraph illustrates a longer chain and how statements can be rearranged to make the content of the chain more cohesive:

My purpose in teaching is for students to learn the material. Sometimes the learning process is difficult and slow. In order for students to learn the material, they must read the textbook. But even when they read the textbook, there is a possibility they won't understand it unless I take the initiative to expand and clarify what they have read. Experience tells me that unless I am conscientious about doing this, students sometimes fail to acquire the learning that is prerequisiteto later learning and at the same time they become confused and discouraged. I simply have to be sure that I help them.

The premises can be written as conditional statements:

1. If I teach, then students will learn the material.
2. If the learning process is difficult and slow, then [the students may become discouraged].
3. If I expect students to know the material, then they must read the textbook.
4. If they read the textbook, then they still may not accurately understand the material.
5. If they do not accurately understand the material, then they may reach inappropriate conclusions.
6. If the conclusions they reach are prerequisite to understanding material later in the course, then they need to understand the textbook.
7. If students do not have prerequisites for later learning, then they may become discouraged.
8. If students become confused and discouraged, then they will not know the material.
   >Students will not learn the material unless I help them.

The premises fit together with more meaning when what would have been premise (2) is moved to become premise (6), since both premises have to do with difficulty and with student discouragement. By making this switch and adding a second premise to each existing premise the argument is extended, but is still linked together in a sound way:

1.0 If I teach, then students will learn the material.
1.1 I teach.
1.2 >Students learn the material.
2.0 If I expect students to learn the material, then they must read the textbook.
2.1 I expect students to learn the material.
2.2 >They must read the textbook.
3.0 If students read the textbook, then they still may not accurately understand the material.
3.1 Students read the textbook.
3.2 >They may not accurately understand the material.
4.0 If students do not accurately understand the material, then they may reach inappropriate conclusions and not have the prerequisites for later learning.
4.1 Students may not accurately understand the material.
4.2 >They may reach inappropriate conclusions and not acquire the prerequisites needed for later learning.
5.0 If students do not reach appropriate conclusions and acquire the prerequisites needed for later learning, then they may become confused and discouraged.
5.1 Students will not acquire the needed prerequisites for later learning by simply reading the textbook.

5.2 >Students may become confused and discouraged.

6.0 If students become confused and discouraged, then the learning process is difficult and slow.

6.1 <u>Students become confused and discouraged.</u>

6.2 >The learning process is difficult and slow.

7.0 If the learning process is difficult and slow even when they read the textbook, then I should help them.

7.1 The learning process is difficult and slow even when they read the textbook.

7.2 >I should help them.

8.0 If I help them by teaching, then they will learn the material.

8.1 <u>I help them by teaching.</u>

8.2 >They learn the material.

Chain reasoning, like all clear, precision thinking, requires careful attention to the conditional relationships between the premises and the conclusion that is reached. If the rules of validity are followed, the reasoning will lead to a logical conclusion.

Applications

1. The following excerpt demonstrates how one classroom teacher has used the above techniques. A second grade teacher, she demonstrates to a group of her peers how to incorporate logic into learning.

TEACHER: Statements in the form of questions: "Now watch while I light this match. Is the wood changing its shape and s i z e ?" (Yes.) "Do you think this is a physical change?" (Maybe.) "But what else is happening?" (I don't have all the wood when it is finished burning. I have a new substance or material.) "What did you see while the match was burning and what do you see now that II have put it out?" (Gas, smoke, vapors, carbon.)

TEACHER: Changes questions into propositions: "When we have a change where new substances are formed, we have a chemical change. Everything on earth is made up of different substances and chemicals. When we heat things or mix things we sometimes change the chemicals in those things." (To teachers wathing the demonstration: "Let the students examine a match. Talk about sulfur and wood. If the class is mature enough, let them light the match and watch it burn. Blow it out after a minute. Examine the carbon. Look at where the sulfur was.")

TEACHER: "Can you think of a time when you saw a chemical change take place? I'll tell you of a few more: When your mom puts cake batter in the oven and bakes it; when you plant a seed and it turns into a plant; and when you eat food and it turns into energy for your body. So a chemical change happens when we actually change the chemicals or substances that make up something."

She then forms a conditional statement and a logical argument. "Look at this candle burning. We could make the following argument:

If the wax and wick change into gases and carbon, then a chemical change is taking place.
The wax is changing into gases and carbon and the wick is changing into carbon.
>A chemical change is taking place."

"The same example is used to demonstrate the biconditional: "We can also say: If and only if...

If and only if the chemicals or substances change into something else, then a chemical change takes place."

She uses the example to further demonstrate the concept of necessary. (She says she does not think second grade students can deal with the concept of sufficient).

"And we can say: In a chemical change, it is necessary for something to change into a different substance."

Chain reasoning with the same students was demonstrated."Students can try chain reasoning by following the statements below:

"If I want to make a chemical change take place, then I must light the candle.
If I light the candle, then the wick will burn.
If the wick burns, then the wax will heat up.
If the wax heats up, then it will turn to gases and carbon .
If the wax turns to gases and carbon, then a_____takes place.
If I light the candle, then a_____takes place."

   a. Write an exercise you can use with the subject matter and the students you teach.

   b. Explain why all reasoning is in a sense deductive.

2. Now commmplete two additional examples:

a. If the subject of a sentence is singular (or plural), then the predicate must also be singular (or plural). Examples: Sam is a fine athlete. Alan and Jane are married.

b. If a noun is used in the nominative case, then the antecedent must be stated in the nominative case. Example: Are you John?

3. Provide an example for each statement below:

    a. If an equation is balanced, then the value is the same on both sides of the equation.

    b. It I want a better world, then I must work toward a better world.

4. Answer each of the following questions:

    a. If little girls are made of "rice and spice and everything nice," then what kind of claim is being made?

    b. If females have less muscular strength in their upper torso than do males, then what kind of claim is being made?

    c. If someone says, "Women are different from men," then what kind of claim is being made?

5. In *The Painted Word,* Tom Wolfe makes the following argument:

If work or a new style disturbed you, it was probably good work. If you hated it, it was probably great....To be against what is new is not to be modern. Not to be modern is to write yourself out of thescene. Not to be in the scene is to be nowhere.

Rewrite the statements as a chain of reasoning, using both Modus Ponens and Modus Tollens.

6. Using Modus Tollens, change the following proposition by G. K. Chesterton into a conditional statement, then into a valid argument:

People generally quarrel because they cannot argue.

See Appendix B for responses.

Chapter 4

Classes and Reasoning

Like many serious disciplines, logic may be studied for its own intrinsic interest or for the purpose of application.

Wesley C. Salmon

We must keep in mind that at the heart of e ducation is the effort to enhance the human capacity to think. . . . Education that attempts only to inculcate good behavior without developing good thinking about behavior cannot be good education.

Thomas Green

Two millenia, from Aristotle to Francis Bacon, were to pass before the processes of inductive reasoning were systematically formulated and emerged as the "the scientific method." Although the unprecedented capability of creating knowledge through inductive reasoning does not stem from Aristotle, our needs for the techniques he developed are becoming more critical as modern technology enables us to generate increasingly more knowledge. Aristotle held the position "that we know by demonstration. By 'demonstration' I mean a scientific syllogism..." Aristotle was primarily seeking understanding, not the scientific genesis of "new" knowledge. He was too much a product of his teacher, Plato, and the tradition from which he came, to fruitfully use what we now universally know as inductive reasoning. But the usefulness of deductive reasoning did not cease with the almost universal reliance on inductive reasoning. Today, when used effectively, deductive reasoning can complement, but not conflict with, inductive reasoning.

In the Information Society, there are at least three questions whichshould be asked about the morass of facts and ideas with which we are continually confronted. One, how is it possible to absorb all the information? Two, how do people sort out what is important, what is contradictory, what can be believed, what is applicable in any given situation; in short, how can people think straight in a sea of words and information? And, three, suppose we manipulate the information in some meaningful way and are thinking straight, how can we clearly communicate messages to others and use them in positive and profitable ways? One way, actually a spin-off from Aristotelian reasoning, is to learn to group information and think in terms of classes.

Classes and Reasoning

Class reasoning is a way of seeing relationships and gaining understanding by creating groups into which subject matter can be sorted. Class reasoning was developed because some subject matter is difficult to examine using only the techniques of sentence reasoning.

A class is a set or group which can be viewed as an entity or a whole. For the most part *we* determine what or who is in a class. A class may be as broad or as narrow as desired. Some examples of classes are animals, mammals, dogs, birds, fish, furniture, chairs, students, teachers, automobiles, males, females, people named Phil. Once a class has been selected, it may be examined in several ways. *All members of a class may be either included or excluded; some members of a class may be either included or excluded ; or some members may be partially included or excluded.*

Suppose someone says, "I like pleasant people, not sore-heads." Immediately two classes have been formed: pleasant people and soreheads. Although the grouping may appear arbitrary and rigid, at one time or another we all probably fit into each group. But suppose someone says, "Mrs. Laffal is the most pleasant teacher on the staff." By using the techniques of class reasoning, we are able to analyze the statement and see the position of Mrs. Laffal relative to all other people and all other teachers on the staff:

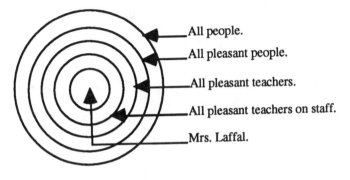

Figure 4.1

There are multiple ways to create classes. In this section, the techniques of using circles to diagram reasoning are used. Logicians, mathematicians and others, often use Euler circles and Venn diagrams to clearly and simplistically convey meaning. The two techniques are the results of the work of the 18th century Swiss mathematician, Leonard Euler, and John Venn, a 19th century British logician. Here the techniques are used without making a distinction between circles and diagrams. In the context of what is being stressed in this book, students need to develop habits of sound reasoning, be able to make proper distinctions within the context of learning subject matter. Using circles can help in the development of such habits.

When using circles, there are at least three possibilities of how statements may be diagrammed: 1) one class is totally included in another; 2) the two classes are entirely separate; and 3) one class is partially included in another class. The essential idea behind the use of circles is to include all members of a class within a circle. Then by relating circles it is possible to graphically demonstrate the relationship of a member of a class to the whole class. For example, suppose someone says that "All A's are B's." Diagrammed using circles, the assertion looks as follows:

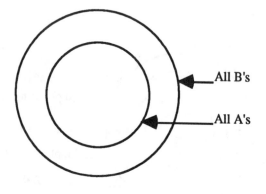

Figure 4. 2

Because the proposition asserts that if something is an A it is therefore totally part of class B, the circle labeled "All B's" represents the class. As diagrammed, it is inescapable that however large or small the group designated as A, every A is at the same time also a B.

If, however, the assertion is that "No A's are B's", the diagram changes:

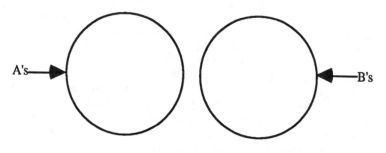

Figure 4.3

Circles A and B do not overlap. To do so would deny the claim that no part of one is any part of the other. But if the assertion is that "Some A's are B's", the diagram changes again:

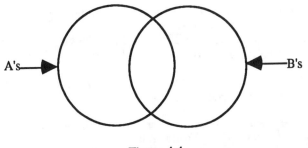

Figure 4.4

In this arrangement, the class labeled A is partially the same as the class labeled B. The area where the circles overlap is the area of sameness. In the areas that do not overlap, the two classes are distinct and apart.

Consider the following statement and how it may be diagrammed using circles: Professor Jones has enjoyed all of Thomas Wolfe's stories.

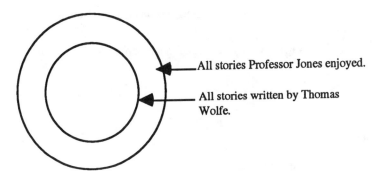

Figure 4.5

The outer circle represents the larger class, all stories Professor Jones has enjoyed. The inner circle represents a smaller class, which is part of the larger class: all of Thomas Wolfe's stories are part of all stories Professor Jones has enjoyed.

In sentence reasoning an argument can be extended to the level of an argument and become specific by turning the first premise into a conditional statement, adding a second premise and reaching a necessary conclusion:

> If professor Jones enjoyed all of Thomas Wolfe's stories, then he enjoyed *Look Homeward Angel.*
> <u>Professor Jones enjoyed all of Thomas Wolfe's stories.</u>
> >Professor Jones enjoyed *Look Homeward Angel.*

Using the techniques of class reasoning, we now see that the argument includes three components:

> The larger class: all stories Professor Jones has enjoyed.
> The smaller class: All of Thomas Wolfe's stories.
> The individual: A specific story by Thomas Wolfe.

Using a system of circles, the three components in the argument can be diagrammed as follows:

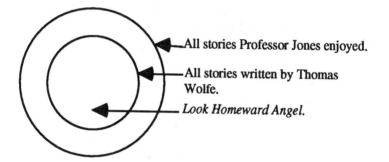

Figure 4.6

Consider another example:

> If all intellectually gifted students are in this class, then Nadine is in this class.
> <u>Nadine is not in this class.</u>
> >Nadine is not intellectually gifted.

Using circles, the argument can be diagrammed:

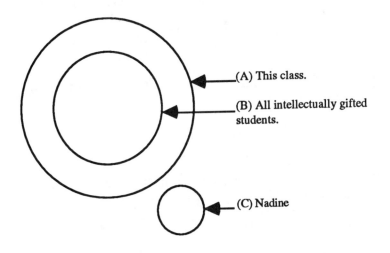

(A) This class.

(B) All intellectually gifted students.

(C) Nadine

Figure 4.7

The conclusion necessarily follows: Nadine is not intellectually gifted. By representing "this class" with A and "all intellectually gifted students" with B, and Nadine with C, the argument is, All B's are A's but C is not an A, therefore, C is not a B.

The key to straight thinking is to work against the conclusion. When the argument is diagrammed it is clear that since Nadine is not in the class where all intellectually gifted students are assigned, therefore, she is not intellectually gifted.

But some arguments are not as clearly and simplistically drawn as those discussed so far. The concept of *some*, as opposed to either*all* or *none*, raises some other important points. To do so, we will introduce another concept: *Universe of Discourse*. A Universe of Discourse represents all possible subjects that can be included in a given argument. By adding a universe of discourse, the argument about Professor Jones and the novels of Thomas Wolfe may be diagrammed another way:

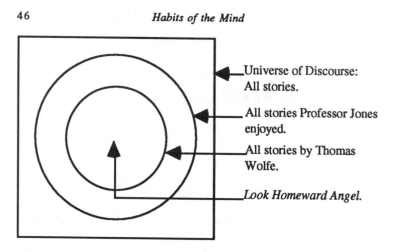

Figure 4.8

If, however, the argument is changed, then the way it may be diagrammed using circles may also change:

If Professor Jones enjoyed some of Thomas Wolfe's stories, then he probably enjoyed *Look Homeward Angel.*
Professor did not enjoy Look Homeward Angel.
>Professor Jones enjoyed some, but not all, of Thomas Wolfe's stories.

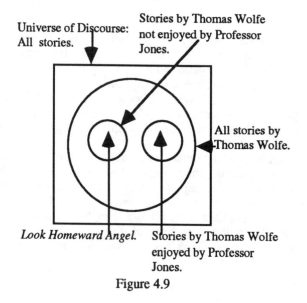

Figure 4.9

Included with the Universe of Discourse are all stories that have ever been written, all the stories Professor Jones has enjoyed, all the stories Thomas Wolfe has written, and the specific story, *Look Homeward Angel*. Since, however, we are interested in infusing the skills and techniques of logic and analysis into the teaching and learning of subject matter, itis now time to discuss logic in learning. Chapter 5 focuses on the ways logic and analysis can be used to create a "new pedagogy. "

Applications

1. Give students a bag of marbles and have them sort the marbles into groups. Do not give them any criteria for sorting. After they finish, have them explain and defend why they sorted the marbles as they did.

2. Into which of the following groups would George Washington not fit? Use the skills of conditional reasoning then give the criteria for your decisions.

   a. Whig
   b. Federalist
   c. Soldier
   d. Statesman

3. Give students six faces (which may be cut out of newspapers and magazines). Have the students stipulate the criteria by which they will group the faces then sort them into classes using *only* the criteria.

Chapter 5

Logic In Learning

To know what excellence is is not enough; we must endeavor to acquire it and to act accordingly.

Aristotle

In general, the proof of a person's knowledge or ignorance is his ability to teach.

Aristotle

To a great extent, intellectual progress is possible because one generation is taught what another finds out. While the claim is not absolute, the implication is difficult to miss - students study and learn the conclusions of other people's reasoning. Students need to possess information, but it is learning to examine and evaluate conclusions for themselves that leads them to understand, to know in the fullest sense.

The late Harvard psychologist, B. F. Skinner, has suggested that a "new pedagogy" is needed in American education. What might constitute a "new pedagogy" needs close examination. Although high level, precision technology has hurled human beings into the Information Age not totally prepared, technological circumstances have not - and probably should not - change the essential purposes of American education. Precision thinking - which can lead to increased rigor, then to increased intellectual ecstasy - is at least one educational key to the future. A generation ago, H. Gordon Hullfish and Philip G. Smith said, "The point is simple: thinking increases the importance of knowledge and skills; it does not diminish it." Two considerations are important. The first is epistemological, how we view knowledge and learning: Is all learning achieved through didactic means or do we use didactic means to enable students to acquire the intellectual skills to learn for themselves? The second consideration is moral: What does one generation owe the next one? In this chapter, the instructional uses of some of the basic concepts and skills from logic are explored. The chapter focuses on the practical uses of the skills of conditional reasoning under the two reasons for teaching logical reasoning which were set forth in chapter 1: 1) *to develop clear, precise thinking skills and 2) to understand the nature of the knowledge.* While these reasons are discussed serially for purposes of writing and teaching, in fact, in learning a synergism results and students often achieve both purposes at the same time.

Purpose: To Develop Clear, Precise Thinking Skills

Suppose we want to use statements about recent historic events to help students understand the world in which they live and at the sametime be able to follow the reasoning of the person who makes the statements? The following example brings these concerns into focus.In a 1990 article in *Foreign Affairs,* the following statements, referring to the fall of the Berlin Wall, were made by Ronald D. Asmus:

> The events of the past year have taught many of us a lesson in humility concerning the remarkable surprises the forces of history can produce. The best guarantees that history will not repeat itself are democracy and Western integration for Germany.

Questioning is a way to begin. Recitation questioning, as noted in chapter 3, can enable the teacher to determine the knowledge levels of students. Analytic questioning can lead to expanded meaning and result in the acquisition of additional intellectual skills. In both the short and the long term, intellectual precision will lead to clear thinking.

Questions and Prior Questions

If one goal of teaching is to cultivate habits of mind that result in students approaching every learning situation from an analytical point of view, questions need to have a specific thrust, be designed to develop a specific meaning. But first, some other techniques of questioning need to be examined.

Any number of questions may be raised about Asmus' commentary on recent history. It is well worth the effort to raise one or more prior questions (sometimes referred to as "metaquestions") which will lead to "clarity before commitment." A prior question is a question which needs to be asked and answered before the question at hand is addressed. Prior questions enable teachers to be sure that the points at issue are focused and unequivocal. Frequently, a prior question will enable the reader to clarify the author's purposes, and perhaps make explicit some of the implicit assumptions underpinning the writer's statements. For example, before asking a broad question, such as, "What are the forces of history?" a discussion of Asmus' statements may be initiated by asking one or more prior questions:

Are there "forces of history"?

If so, then do we have cause to believe that we learn valuable lessons from the forces of history?

If there are lessons in history, then are the lessons certain or only indicators, guideposts to what may occur in the future?

If history is different from other subject matter, such as chemistry, mathematics and foreign language, then in what ways is it different?

Prior questions narrow the focus and put the lesson into clear perspective. After prior questions have been asked and answered, then the questions directly focusing on the subject at hand can be addressed. When utilized, analytic questioning can achieve at least three objectives:

1. Narrow the focus of the question so that specific points can be understood;

2. Use the skills of logic and analytic philosophy to analyze the "narrowed" question, and

3. Reach a reasonable, supportable conclusion (synthesis).

A number of recitation questions may flow from a consideration of Asmus' statements:

If the events of the past year have taught us humility, then to which of these events does the author refer?

If we are to learn some lessons, then what are they?

If the forces of history have produced examples of surprises, then what are they?

If Asmus bases the statement that democracy and the Western integration of Germany are guarantees that history will not repeat itself, then on what does he base the assertion?

Recitation questioning should lead to analytical questioning:

If we have learned from the events of the past year, then why does the author say the lessons that have been learned are lessons in humility?

If the author uses the term "humility," then is he using it in the way it is ordinarily used?

If Asmus uses the expression, "forces of history," then to what is he referring? If Asmus believes "history repeats itself," then how does he support the claim?

If Asmus refers to "Western integration," then to what is he pointing?

If left as "how," "what, "and "why" questions, a perplexing degree of ambiguity remains. The perplexity can, however, be reduced. by moving from questions to propositions to conditional statements then to arguments.

From Statements to Arguments

Consider the question, What does Asmus mean by "history repeats itself"? First, convert the question to a proposition. The change can be accomplished by simply converting the question to a declarative statement: History repeats itself. Now the sentence can be tested against the criteria of true or false, right or wrong.

Second, convert the proposition to a conditional statement. The conversion can be achieved by stating, "If history repeats itself, then..." Now the consequent can either be provided by the teacher or the students can add their own. Either way, thinking becomes focused. Students are now faced with stating then finding support for the consequences of the belief that history does or does not repeat itself. This task is far more specific than searching for an answer to the speculative, elusive "why"?

Third, turn the conditional statement into an argument. When a consequent is added to the conditional stem, and a second premise is added, the two premises can be related either by affirming the antecedent (Modus Ponens) or by denying the consequent (Modus Tollens), and a necessary conclusion will follow:

If history repeats itself, then we can accurately predict the future.
History repeats itself.
>We can accurately predict the future.

This is a focused, valid Modus Ponens argument. Based on the premises, the conclusion is the only one that can be reached. Now that validity has been established the quest for truth can be pursued. But students need more to know how to pursue truth.

Sometimes, students are unclear about specifically what they are to learn. Is it information? The meaning of information? The relationship of the information to other information? The relationship of the information to other academic disciplines, to events, to people? Or something else? Being clear about the goals of any learning task is a critical part of learning. Sometimes learning misfires and future learning which may be premised upon the assumption that current lessons have been learned is also jeopardized. To initiate students into the intellectual habits of thinking clearly, the same steps that were used above can be taken. In this case, our focus shifts from the question of whether or not history repeats itself to the lessons in humility Asmus says we have learned from events of "the past year." First, the question is changed to a proposition. As it turns out, Asmus' original statement is a proposition:

The events of the past year have taught many of us a lesson in humility concerning the remarkable surprises the forces of history can produce.

Now the proposition is converted to a conditional statement:

If many of us have learned lessons in humility about the remarkable surprises the forces of history produce, then we learned these lessons as a result of the events of the past year.

When a second premise is added and a conclusion reached, an argument is made:

If we have learned lessons about surprises in the forces of history, then we learned these lessons as a result of the events of the past year.
We have learned lessons about surprises in the forces of history.
>We learned them from the events of the past year.

Students can now deal with the task of identifying the events of the year in question that focus on the "forces of history," whatever these forces turn out to be. When such tasks are combined with the tasks embedded in other questions, the impact of the statements begins to emerge. Other questions may be: Why might the author believe in the "forces of history"? How will the democratization and integration of Germany into Western Europe help avoid "history repeating itself"? and What does the author mean by *integration?* The statements now have not only a subject matter context, but a reasoning context as well, and the quest for truth goes on.

Purpose: Understand the Nature of the Knowledge

Asmus either states or implies that there are forces in history and that history repeats itself. Both statements say something about the unique nature of the discipline of history. Does anyone ever say, "Chemistry repeats itself"? or "The forces of mathematics"? Since such statements are not made about any other discipline, but it is quite common to hear either or both statements made about history, what is unique about the discipline of history that prompts such statements? Students can wrestle with these questions, in a precise format, by restating the propositions as conditional statements:

If there are forces of history, then these forces can be identified.

If history repeats itself, then unambiguous examples of this phenomenon can be found.

Conditional statements, such as these, are rich in discussion and research possibilities. The focus becomes sharper, however, when additional steps are taken and the statements become arguments:

If there are forces in history, then these forces can be identified.
There are forces in history.
>These forces can be identified.

If *history repeats itself*, then unambiguous examples of this phenomenon can be found.
History repeats itself.
>Unambiguous examples of this phenomenon can be found.

By moving from propositions to arguments, the meaning of the premises becomes clear and unequivocal. We are now in a position to investigate the claims that *forces of history* exist and that *history repeats itself.* There will still be a great deal about the nature of the discipline of history that the students will not know. But that students emerge with a definitive understanding of history as a discipline is not the point. A scholar may spend a career wrestling with such questions. That they emerge as students who think with more precision, that the subject matter they are expected to master is in some ways clear to them, and that they have at least some insight into the relationship of historical knowledge to other knowledge are important learning considerations that we ignore at the expense of students' futures.

In the following section, how the skills of logic can be incorporated into teaching is discussed further. Examples are given using the opening paragraph of the *Declaration of Independence* . Following this discussion, a variety of examples of subject matter are given to indicate the wide applications the techniques of logic have to teaching.

A Case Study: Declaration of Independence

"The Unanimous Declaration of the Thirteen United States of America" was presented "In Congress" on July 4, 1776. Written byThomas Jefferson of Virginia, the opening sentence is equivalent to a statement of purpose:

When, in the course of human events, it becomes necessary for one people to dissolve the political bands which have connected them to another, and to assume, among the powers of the earth, the separate and equal station to which the laws of nature and of nature's God entitle them, a decent respect to the opinions of mankind requires that they should declare the causes which impel them to the separation.

Continuing to use the purposes for learning with which we began in chapter 1, the analysis proceeds in the same sequence which was developed earlier: convert sentences to propositions, propositions to conditional statements and conditional statements to arguments.

Purpose: To Develop Clear, Precise Thinking Skills

Historically, American education has focused on teaching and learning the conclusions generated by inductive reasoning. But it is not sufficient simply to teach students the conclusions that someone else has reached through the processes of inductive reasoning. *Knowing that* and *knowing how* should both be goals for all students.

Professor Thomas Green, a longtime logician, epistemologist and teacher, states unequivocally that "all reasoning, without exception, is built around the structure of conditional reasoning." "The manners of teaching are the manners of argument," he says. It follows then that the "manners of argument" are also the manners of learning. Precision teaching may not be either sufficient to or guarantee precision learning in every instance, but precision teaching may be *necessary* to precision learning. The following discussion illustrates how the skills of logic can become the skills of learning, as students develop the habits of clear, precision thinking.

Sentences to Propositions

Jefferson's statement is grounded in one or more unstated assumptions. Hidden assumptions can frequently be recognized by asking prior questions:

> If one nation is to take its place among the nations of the world, then is it always necessary to throw off the political bands that bind it to another nation?

> If such an assumption is accepted, then is there historical precedent for the assumption?

> If Jefferson had wished to rest his case on grounds other than history, then on what may he have rested it?

Jefferson's long sentence embraces a number of thoughts. By treating the several thoughts as if they are individual sentences, each thought can be turned into a separate proposition:

Sometimes it is necessary for one people to dissolve the political bonds they have with another people and assume an equal station among the peoples of the earth.

The laws of nature and nature's God entitle them to such a station.

A decent respect for the opinions of mankind requires that "one people" state what caused them to separate themselves from another.

Propositions to Conditional Statements

These propositions can now be turned into conditional statements:

> If human events require it, then one people should dissolv the political bands which connect them to another, separate themselves and assume the place to which they are entitled.

> If the laws of nature and nature's God entitle the "one people" to assume an equal station among the powers of the earth, then they should assume such a station.

If the "one people" have a decent respect for the opinions of mankind, then they should declare the causes that impel them to separation.

Conditional Statements to Arguments

By adding a second premise to each conditional statement then reaching the necessary conclusion, valid deductive arguments are created. It is important that students continually be reminded that the quest for validity should always precede the quest for truth:

If human events require it, then people should dissolve the bands that connect them to another, separate themselves and take the place to which they are entitled.
Human events require it.
>Then the people should dissolve the bands that connect them to another, separate themselves and assume the place to which they are entitled.

If the laws of nature entitle "one people" an equal station among the powers of the earth, then they should assume such a station. The laws of nature entitle them to assume an equal station among the powers of the earth.
>They should assume such a station.

If the "one people" have a decent respect to the opinions of mankind, then they should declare the causes that impel them to the separation. They have a decent respect to the opinions of mankind.
>They declare the causes that impel them to separation.

These arguments are valid and can be tested further.

Necessary and sufficient

In all conditional reasoning the following two questions can be asked: 1) Is the truth of the antecedent *sufficient* to guarantee the truth of the consequent? and 2) Is the truth of the consequent *necessary* to guarantee the truth of the antecedent? A necessary condition for the occurrence of an event is a circumstance in whose *absence* the event cannot occur. A sufficient condition for the occurrence of an event is a circumstance in which the event *must* occur. Necessary and sufficient conditions can be demonstrated using Jefferson's statement:

If human events require it, then one people should dissolve the
political bonds that connect them to another, separate themselves and
assume the place to which they are entitled.
Human events require it.
>One people should dissolve the political bonds that connect them to
another, separate themselves and assume the place to which they are
entitled.

The antecedent - "If human events require it" - is sufficient to
guarantee the truth of the consequent, provided the world is viewed the
way Jefferson saw it when he wrote the statement. Jefferson, the entire
committee appointed to write the Declaration and the Continental
Congress, intellectually and emotionally, appear to have believed that
human events were *sufficient* cause for the colonists to separate
themselves from England. Given the truth of what "human events
require," the actions stated in the consequent *had* to occur. And the
truth of the consequent is necessary to guarantee the truth of the
antecedent. In the absence of the antecedent, the actions stated in the
consequent cannot have occurred. Without the human capability to
examine and evaluate "human events" there is no way we can argue that
the statement of the need to separate from Britain could have been made.
Both the necessary and sufficient conditions are met. As we have seen,
when an argument meets the conditions of necessary and sufficient, it
can be written as a biconditional.

The Biconditional

When the arguments from the Declaration of Independence are written
as biconditionals, they look as follows:

One people should dissolve the political bands that connect them
to another, *if and only if* they are willing to separate themselves and
assume the place to which they are entitled.

The "one people" should assume such a station, *if and only if* the laws
of nature and of nature's God entitle them to assume an equal station
among the powers of the earth.

The "one people" should declare the causes that impel them to separate
themselves from another *if and only if* they have a decent respect to
the opinions of mankind.

Based on the three biconditionals, a series of questions can be raised to
stimulate reasoning. To the first biconditional:

Q. If the colonists resolved to dissolve the political bands that connected them to England, then how can we know this?

A. They separated themselves and assumed their station among the powers of the earth.

To the second biconditional:

Q. If the colonists assumed they had a right to take their station among the powers of the earth, then how can we know this?

A. Their actions demonstrated that they believed that nature and nature's God entitled them to do so.

To the third biconditional:

Q. If the colonists had a decent respect for mankind, then how can we know this?

A. They declared the causes that impelled them to take the actions they took.

A series of additional questions can further guide the inquiry:

If Jefferson says "one" people instead of "a" people, then to what do we attribute the change from Locke's wording?

If Jefferson says such an action was "necessary," then on what does he rest the claim of necessity?

If Jefferson uses the expression "political bands, " then to what is he referring?

If Jefferson refers to "the powers of the earth," then to which powers of the time may he have been alluding?

If Jefferson says,"the laws of nature and of nature's God, then to whom or what is he referring?

If this is a truth claim, then what type of claim is it?

If Jefferson's statements are true, then are any of them either analytic or metaphysical?

Using Chain Reasoning

In Jefferson's long sentence, a number of important lessons in reasoning are illustrated. For instance, the sentence is an example of chain reasoning. For purposes of convenience, it is stated again:

> When in the course of human events, it becomes necessary for one people to dissolve the political bands which have connected them with another, and to assume, among the powers of the earth, the separate and equal station to which the laws of nature and nature's God entitle them, a decent respect to the opinions of mankind requires that they should declare the causes which impel them to the separation.

From this sentence, a sequence of propositions can be generated:

> In the course of human events, it sometimes becomes necessary for one people to dissolve the political bands that connect them to another.

> It is also sometimes necessary for those same people to assume aseparate and equal station among the powers of the earth.

> Nature and nature's God impel the people to this station.

> A decent respect for mankind requires those people to declare why they shave chosen to separate themselves.

To facilitate precision thinking, a second premise may be added to each of the four conditional statements and conclusions to each set of premises reached. The four premises then add up to the one basic conclusion with which the argument began: "When in the course of human events it becomes necessary for one people to dissolve..."

> If in the course of human events, it becomes necessary, then one people should dissolve the political bands that connect them with another.
> <u>In the course of human events it became necessary.</u>
> >One people dissolved the political bands that connected them with another.

> If such a people choose to dissolve the political bands that connect them to another, then they must accept a separate and equal station among the powers of the earth.
> The people choose to dissolve the political bands that connect them <u>with another.</u>
> >Then they must accept a separate and equal station among the powers of the earth.

If the people accept the separate and equal station among the powers of the earth, then they are impelled to do so by nature and nature's God. The people accept a separate and equal station among the powers of the earth.
>They are impelled to do so by nature and nature's God.

If they are impelled to do so by nature and nature's God, then a decent respect for mankind requires that they declare why they have chosen to separate themselves.
They are impelled to do so by nature and nature's God.
>They show a decent respect for mankind by declaring the causes that impels them to separate.

Using Class Reasoning

Marzano reports that a group of middle school students outlined the logic of the *Declaration of Independence* in the following way.

(A) Governments that should be supported, (B) protect the rights of people to life, liberty and the pursuit of happiness, (C) government of George III did not protect the God-given rights of the people. There fore, the government of George III was not, and should not have been supported.

Using symbols, the reasoning is as follows:

All A is B.
C is not B.
Therefore, C is not A.

When the argument is diagramed using circles, it looks as follows:

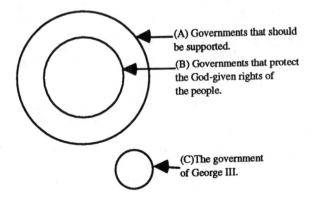

(A) Governments that should be supported.

(B) Governments that protect the God-given rights of the people.

(C)The government of George III.

Figure 5.1

The argument ends with a conclusion: The government of George III did not deserve to be supported. The diagram demonstrates the validity of the conclusion. George III's government was completely outside the rationale that buttresses Jefferson's argument for when a government should be supported.

The reasoning in the opening statement in the *Declaration of Independence* can also be diagrammed in other ways:

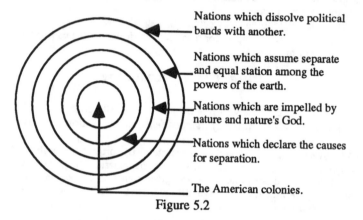

Nations which dissolve political bands with another.

Nations which assume separate and equal station among the powers of the earth.

Nations which are impelled by nature and nature's God.

Nations which declare the causes for separation.

The American colonies.

Figure 5.2

Figure 5.2 demonstrates that any nation that dissolves political bands with another nation is a nation which also assumes a separate and equal station among the powers of the earth. When a nation assumes a separate and equal station among the powers of the earth, it is impelled to do so by nature and nature's God. If a nation is impelled to take this step, then that nation has a responsibility to declare the causes for the separation. The colonies saw themselves as such a nation. When students can reason this way with clarity and precision they will more readily learn the subject matter.

Clarification of subject matter may have different meanings for different people. Clarification may mean the unraveling of complicated, hard-to-grasp material; or the enhancement of what is included in a lesson by the addition of new, related information; or the understanding of terminology and the context in which it is used; or how the subject matter fits into a larger context, such as how a sentence fits into a paragraph; or how the history of a state fits into the history of the nation; or yet something else. Circumstances, including the academic progress of the students and the purposes of the lesson, help determine how the concept of clarification is viewed and used by a teacher. In any case, clarification is a crucial concept, one that should be accounted for in a deliberate way.

In the two examples which follow, the skills of logic are used to hone, refine and clarify the purposes of the *Declaration of Independence* as reflected in separate statements by Benjamin Franklin and Thomas Jefferson.

From Benjamin Franklin

Upon the adoption of the *Declaration of Independence* by the Continental Congress, Dr. Franklin made what has become a well-known statement:

We must all hang together now or most assuredly we shall all hangseparately.

Franklin's statement is a proposition. The statement is not, however, explicitly worded as a conditional statement, even though implicitly the sense of "if, then" is there. By changing the wording slightly, the statement can be made into an explicit conditional statement and at the same time retain the sense of Dr. Franklin's observation:

If we do not all hang together now, then we shall all most assuredly hang separately.

By adding a second premise, and reaching a conclusion, the conditional statement becomes a conditional argument. The technique of Modus Tollens - denying the consequent - is used:

If we do not all hang together now, then we shall all most assuredly hang separately.
We shall not all most assuredly hang separately.
>We shall all hang together now.

Students may get more involved by first pursuing recitation questions, followed by analysis questions:

What evidence can be found to either confirm or deny that the writers of the *Declaration of Independence,* members of the Congress and the colonies "hung together" to avoid "hanging separately"? Where can we find such evidence?

How can we know that the evidence gathered is either necessary or sufficient, or both, to support the conclusion?

If the tests of necessary and sufficient are applied and are found to be affirmative, then the statement can be turned into a biconditional:

If, and only if, we hang together now shall we avoid hanging together later.

When we use the disjunctive rule our reasoning is "either, or," but not both. Without in any way modifying either the meaning or the impact of Franklin's assertion, we may restate it as follows.

We must either all hang together now or most assuredly we shall all hang separately.

First, a number of clarifying questions may be raised to focus thinking and increase precision in thinking:

In what two ways does Franklin use the word "hang"? (See chapter 8 for information on using words ambiguously.)

Are the two choices Franklin identifies mutually exclusive?

If an individual colonial citizen chose to hang together how would this decision avoid hanging separately?

If an individual citizen chose not to hang together how would this decision have increased the likelihood that he or she might hang separately?

Of what importance are Franklin's uses of the terms "all" and "separately""?

Does the meaning of the statement shift if "all" is changed to "some" and "separately" is changed to "singly"?

Using circles, the choices are diagrammed:

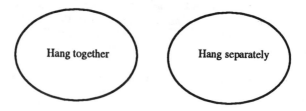

Figure 5.3

Citizens of the colonies had to make an either/or decision. They did.

From Thomas Jefferson

Since the time of the writing of the *Declaration of Independence,* we have recognized that Jefferson borrowed ideas and even wording from the English physician, teacher and philosopher, John Locke. Locke's *Second Treatise on Government* was written in the late 17th century. Jefferson chose to paraphrase some of Locke's statements rather than use them directly. For example, in the second paragraph Jefferson states that among the unalienable rights of man is the right to "life, liberty, and the pursuit of happiness." Locke had said that "life, liberty, and property" are the unalienable rights of human beings. Jefferson broadened the concept and at the same time made the statement appear a bit less self-serving, by changing "property" to "the pursuit of happiness."

What we may assume Jefferson's intention to be can be viewed as a conjunctive statement. By examining the following conditional statement, which remains true to Jefferson's assertion, the two-pronged "both" becomes clear:

If human beings have unalienable rights, then among these rights are life, liberty and the pursuit of happiness.

The conditional statement carries the same meaning as, "If human beings have unalienable rights, then they have the right to both life, liberty and the pursuit of happiness."

Jefferson made another noticeable change in Locke's wording. Locke said "a" people; Jefferson changed the "a" to "one" people. Perhaps he did so to emphasize the unity of purpose that he thought necessary for the separate and at that time sovereign colonies to assume if they were to successfully unite and achieve their independence from Great Britain. This point can be examined through inquiry that begins with the following conditional statement:

If Jefferson changed "a" people to "one" people, then he did so because...

Students can complete the conditional statement, based on what they either know, believe or suspect to be true. The statement can then be turned into an argument. The students' task then becomes finding reliable information that will either confirm or deny what they have argued. In effect, they will ferret out one of Jefferson's basic assumptions.

Once the question of truth has been established, the argument can be examined using other techniques:

Is what Jefferson asserted both necessary and sufficient?

How does the statement read when stated as a biconditional?

Is the biconditional accurate in view of everything else that is known about the times and circumstances?

What can be learned that will further clarify Jefferson's statement that he was writing "The Unanimous Declaration"?

Purpose: Understand the Nature of the Knowledge

Most knowledge in most disciplines is both tentative and ephemeral. It is tentative because the knowledge is generated using the inductive model of reasoning. Knowledge that results from setting up and testing hypotheses is always subject to revision and reinterpretation. Even what have been long considered as scientific laws sometimes change. The demise of Newtonian physics illustrates this point. Nature hasn't changed, but what human beings know about nature and how it works, and the skills that have been developed to probe and study it, have changed. Knowledge is ephemeral because it often does not last forever. Changes in circumstances, such as technological advancements or new knowledge that either obviates previously known information or causes it to become obsolete or more or less important, can change what was once known to be true into something that is no longer true.

Students - even very young students - should be introduced to the nature of the knowledge they are studying. How did it become knowledge? How is it different from other knowledge in other disciplines? How does it relate to other disciplines? Why is knowledge different in different disciplines? Why do we study the disciplines? Is all knowledge used the same way? These, and related questions, can contribute to the fullness of student understanding and to the intellectual satisfaction to be derived from studying and learning. By gaining an understanding of the nature of the discipline being taught (or from which information that is being taught is derived) the teacher can help students sense and ultimately understand that academic disciplines have a "personality," not too unlike the way individuals and institutions have personalities.

Questions

An examination of the nature of the knowledge being taught can begin with a series of questions:

Why do people in the 1990s need to know about the *Declaration of Independence?*

How important is the *Declaration of Independence* in the history of the nation?

How do we determine what is important?

Do American's today still believe, as Thomas Paine asserted in *Common Sense*, in 1776, that Englishmen were persuaded that monarchy was an acceptable form of government only because "history [was] stuffed with fables"?

Students can turn these questions into propositions which will lead them to both investigate and to reason:

People in the 1990s need to know about the *Declaration of Independence.*

The *Declaration of Independence* is one of the most important documents in American history.

Paine asserted that Englishmen were duped into accepting monarchy by means of "history stuffed with fables."

Propositions can then be turned into conditional statements:

If people in the 1990s do not know about the *Declaration of Independence*, then...

If the *Declaration of Independence* is important in American history, then...

If Thomas Paine said that Englishmen were duped into accepting a monarchy by means of "history stuffed with fables," then he said so because..

By writing a consequent to each of these antecedent statements, students learn how to make an "educated guess" based on 1) whatever other knowledge they have of the events in question and 2) what seems most reasonable. Conditional statements can then be turned into arguments:

> If people in the 1990s do not know about the *Declaration of Independence,* then...
> People in the 1990s don't know about the *Declaration of Independence.*
> >

> If the *Declaration of Independence is* important in American history, then...
> The *Declaration of Independence* is important in American history.
> >

> If Thomas Paine thought that Englishmen were duped into accepting a monarchy by means of "history stuffed with fables," then he thought sobecause...
> Paine thought Englishmen had been duped into accepting monarchy by means of "history stuffed with fables."
> >

In the process, students also learn lessons such as those captured in the following questions:

If your responses to the above arguments lead you to accept or reject the belief of the Greeks that h istory is cyclical, thenon what do you base your responses?
If you want to test whether or not Paine was correct in his view of history, then how would you develop an argument to do so?

If the following statement is true, "The *Declaration of Independence* has turned out to be one of the two or three most enduring and influential documents of modern times, then how can either confirm or deny the claim?

Examples are instructive, but not necessarily definitive. Neither one example nor one lesson will result in students thoroughly understanding the nature of the knowledge, but no one example has to do so. Inquiry is limited only by imagination and a dearth of knowledge and skills. The techniques and skills used to this point will be continued as we examine language and the use of language in teaching and learning in Chapter 6.

Chapter 6

Language

All things excellent are as difficult as they are rare.

Spinoza

...it is wrong to say that a good language is important to good thought; it is the essence of it.

Charles Sanders Peirce

Language is the natural form of knowledge. A theory of knowledge must consequently begin with a theory of language.

Reichenbach

When we reason we use language. And when we critique reasoning we are at the same time critiquing language since language is the medium through which reasoning is expressed. In the 17th century, Leibnitz set the tone for the modern world when he said, "I truly believe that languages are the best mirror of the human mind, and that an exact analysis of the meanings of words would reveal the operations of the understanding far better than anything else."

Modern thinkers, from diverse fields, agree with Leibnitz. A modern scholar, Noam Chomsky, also refers to language as a "mirror of the mind." Language, Chomsky argues, helps us understand the specifics of human intelligence. John Stuart Mill contends, "Language is evidently, and by admission of all philosophers, one of the principal instruments or helps of thought; and any imperfection in the instrument, or in the mode of employing it, is confessedly liable still more than in almost any other art, to confuse and impede the process, and destroy all ground of confidence in the result." In the field of public policy, the late-19th century Indiana senator, William Ian Beardmore Beveridge, once said, "Careful and correct use of language is a powerful aid to straight thinking, for putting into words precisely what we mean necessitates getting our own minds quite clear on what we mean."

What we think, what we know, what we want others to know and do, are usually communicated through language. "We cannot habitually speak a language and be unaffected by it," Green says. When students are striving to learn precise thinking skills, their abilities to do so should not be hampered by garbled, imprecise uses of language, especially by teachers. Ludwig Wittgenstein, the Austrian philosopher who spent much of his life in Great Britain, was not being totally cynical when he said, "Philosophy is a battle against the bewitchment of our intelligence by means of language." The British philosopher, John Wilson, points out a reality to which every teacher should be sensitive: "Instead of using language, we are in a very real sense used by it; we allow words to guide our thinking, instead of guiding our own thinking consciously or critically."

But language and communications are not necessarily the same. Individuals must share a language in order to communicate through the language. By sharing a language people share the same concepts, the same understandings, the same sensitivity to tone and accent, the same subtle nuances. Nevertheless, in the world of Everyman, as well as in the classroom, individuals frequently "talk past each other." A topic of discussion in the abstract may be the same in the mind of every party to a discussion, but either the context in which the discussion occurs, the use of terms, or sometimes the deliberate intent to either befuddle, impress or amaze, can defeat clear communication.

Wittgenstein dwelled at such length on the relationship of language to reasoning that today academics attribute to him the expression, "ordinary language philosophy," meaning the language of Everyman. But ordinary language is not necessarily an ordinary concept. Given the number of words in the working vocabularies of most human beings, the way words are used and the context in which they are expected to convey messages, it is hardly surprising that miscommunications occur. America's first public school superintendent, Horace Mann, lists "a fertile mind" and "mastery of language" as the two criteria necessary to becoming educated. Language, he says, is "the gateway to the subjects of the common school curriculum." And the curriculum is taught using ordinary language.

Semanticists, etymologists and language teachers all have specific reasons for studying language. And everyone has varied purposes for using language. The Irish-born philosopher, George Berkeley, in his *Treatise Concerning the Principles of Human Knowledge* , said "...the communicating of ideas...is not the chief and only end of language, as is commonly supposed. There are other ends, as the raising of some passion, the exciting to or deterring from an action, the putting the mind in some particular disposition..." As a rule, language is used to achieve one of four purposes: 1) to evaluate, either ethically, aesthetically or pragmatically; 2) to command or direct; 3) to express emotions; and 4) to inform. In this chapter, three ways in which language is employed to achieve these four purposes, the use of definitions, metaphors and slogans, are examined.

Definitions

Without the definition of words, it would be impossible to communicate with clarity, precision and understanding. Dewey reminds us that misunderstandings are likely to result to the degree that a word is used differently by two different cultures. Definitions enable us to reduce "the pitfalls laid by language in the way of the thinker."

To further reduce the pitfalls on the road to understanding, we must grasp the importance of Wittgenstein's widely accepted, unequivocal, guideline: "The meaning of a word is its use in the language." "For not to have one meaning is to have no meaning and if words have no meaning, all discussions with one another and even, strictly speaking, with ourselves, is over, since we cannot think at all if we do not think of one thing...", Aristotle says. Not uncommonly, people tacitly assume that words have intrinsic or magic meanings. "It has always meant that," we hear. For well over fifty years, Reichenbach has reminded us that "a communicative function begins only when there are certain rules established for the use of the terms." To accent the notion that words have intrinsic meanings, the British philosopher J. L. Austin maintains that "the meaning of a word is a spurious phrase."

A popular stratagem, the dysfunctional consequences of which sometimes go unrecognized, is reflected in the assertion that "the first thing we need to do is define our terms." In many cases definition, as an initial step, may be in order. But to begin by defining terms and then expect that either the discussion and analysis will be restricted to the definition that has been asserted or that by fiat of definition all barriers to congeniality and agreement will be removed, can restrict rather than facilitate reasoning. Unless the functions of definition are understood, they can serve as argument stoppers rather than as a means to clarity and understanding. Some examples are helpful.

In international affairs the importance of definitions is often gravely serious. Winston Churchill recalls a conversation at Potsdam in 1945 in which he asked Marshall Stalin, "What is meant by Germany?" Stalin replied that he did not define Germany as being a united nation any longer. If Germany was to be defined as one country, after World War II, then "united" would have to mean under the control of the U. S. S. R., Stalin said. Stalin's definition obviated the likelihood that further discussion would lead to a more positive and functional agreement among Western nations and the Soviet Union. Earlier in 1945, at Yalta, perhaps foreseeing the difficulties ahead, Churchill had reflected on the imperative for the allied leaders to use the same terms in the same ways. "This was the test case between us and the Russians of the meaning of such terms as democracy, sovereignty, independent, representative Government [sic], and free and unfettered elections," Churchill said.

Neither physicians, attorneys, engineers, educators, nor pool players function well without sharing a common set of terms, with prior agreement on what the terms are used to mean. The need for a common vocabulary among educators is critical. Definitions presuppose rather than replace critical analysis. There are, Aristotle says, two parts to any definition: 1) a general group to which a word is assigned, and 2) an expression of how the word is different within the group. For example, *animal* is a group and *dog is* a specific use of a word to indicate a species of animal. *Collie* dog is even more specific.

There are many ways definitions can be grouped. The discussion in the remainder of the chapter uses the groupings suggested by Israel Scheffler, Professor Emeritus of the Harvard Graduate School. Scheffler labels definitions as *stipulative, descriptive* and *programmatic*. The labels are arbitrary, but the groupings are functional.

Stipulative Definitions

With great confidence, Humpty Dumpty asserted that words mean what he says they mean, even though Alice weakly protested that he used words in many different ways. But Humpty Dumpty insisted that he was the master of how he used words. Like Humpty Dumpty, the user of a *stipulative definition* is the master of its usage, and therefore the master of its meaning. When a definition for a word is either invented to fulfill a specific need or is used in a narrower sense than is typically the case a commonly accepted and useful technique is to *stipulate* a definition. To stipulate is to clearly state how a word or expression is being used in the immediate context. Stipulative definitions can reduce ambiguity and improve understanding.

When Samuel Johnson, the 18th century English man of letters and connoisseur of words, defines "lexicographer" - which was his profession - as "a maker of dictionaries; a harmless drudge," he is partially speaking tongue-in-cheek. In a light-hearted way, he uses a stipulative definition. Johnson may have been offended if someone else had referred to a lexicographer as a drudge, but the example is instructive. In every culture in the world, stipulative definitions are used. The practice is ancient. In the *Nicomachean Ethics* Aristotle stipulates his use of the word *emotions:* "By emotions I mean desire, anger, fear, pride, envy, joy, love, hatred, regret, ambition, pity - in a word, whatever feeling is attended by pleasure or pain."

Stipulative definitions are not difficult to find. For example, it is not just occasionally that the word "professional" is used in modern society. Many people work long and hard to be professionals. The term is used with great breadth of coverage. Even so, rarely is the question of what is meant raised. The lack of precision leaves us with an unclear view of what is meant, who is a professional and who is not. Most Americans will list physicians, attorneys, and perhaps accountants and engineers, as "professionals." But what about football, baseball, hockey and basketball players who also are paid for their services? What about actors, writers, career military personnel, college professors and elementary and secondary school teachers? What makes one occupation "professional" and another not professional? Does use of the term "professional" indicate that all professionals operate at the same level of performance, or get comparable remuneration, or are highly respected (or feared) in the community, or have the same status, or educational background, or degree of specialization?

A modern professor of philosophy, Bruce Wilshire, confronts the question of who is a professional by stipulating a definition for how he uses the term: "To put it precisely: by 'professionalism' I mean a way of life which provides a livelihood through the practice of a skill valued by society; this requires a 'cognitive base' of expert knowledge which can be acquired only through protracted training in a special field. The term also connotes the discipline necessary to exercise the skill whenever required." Implicit in Wilshire's definition are criteria by which professionalism can be judged: a way of life, remuneration, a skill that requires a high level of training, a skill that is valued by society, a special field, and the discipline to practice the skill as well as acquire it. We may, of course, disagree with his stipulations. For instance, would either prostitutes, drug dealers or assassins be included in Wilshire's use of the term "professional"?" Each group seems to meet his criteria.

Is teaching a profession? The answer may be found in another rhetorical-sounding, but provocative series of questions: How do teachers want to be defined? By the level of training and skill? By their value to society? By the sense of responsibility displayed in the discharge of their duties? By the level of remuneration? By the status and respect granted by society? By the independence of movement afforded by the nature of the work? Some of these criteria are applicable to teachers, some are not. And the questions bring into focus the folly of blanket comparisons between differing occupational groups. Groups such as teachers who work for a bureaucracy do not have the freedom of movement of entreprenuers who set up their own business organizations. Neither do teachers have the same potential level of remuneration enjoyed by fee-takers. Do the differences make teachers less professional than physicians and attorneys? How a term is used, that is, the criteria by which a term is judged, is its definition.

Dewey ;meticulously defines his use of the word naturalistic: "As it is here employed it means, on one side, that there is no breach of continuity between operations of inquiry and biological operations and physical operations." Occasionally, we hear someone .i.stipulate ;what, in his or her mind characterizes a "real man": strong, self-assured, patient, courageous, gentle, willing to fight for what he believes, et al. In every case, the speaker tells us how terms are being used, and at the same time stipulates the criteria used to judge whether or not the conditions of the definitions have been met.

Stipulative definitions do not reflect popular usage. When a word is used in the popular or everyday sense, the sense in which it is defined in a dictionary, stipulation is not needed. By their very nature stipulative definitions are not difficult to recognize. For instance, in *Historians' Fallacies*, David Hackett Fischer is painstakingly obvious about his usage: "In this book an *event* is understood as any past happening. A *fact* is a true descriptive statement about past events. To *explain* is merely to make plain, clear, or understandable some problem about past events, so that the resulting knowledge will be useful in dealing with future problems. An explanatory *paradigm* is the active structure of workable questions and the factual statements which are adduced to answer them."

The lack of precise meaning comes when a word or phrase is used in a way that is subject to more than one meaning but a specific usage is not made clear. When we recognize the effects that the ambiguous, unclear use of words can have in such areas as international affairs the importance of stipulative definitions becomes serious. Writing about the Vietnam War, David Halberstam, in *The Best and the Brightest*, discusses the different meanings attributed to the word *stability* by the Americans and the South Vietnamese in the early 1960s:

Stability, that was the key word, to bring stability to that land, though stability as we defined it was colonialism as the Vietnamesedefined it. Freedom to them was instability and revolution. Just asthe policy had gotten turned around, so too had the words; as our policy had become an aberration, so too, and this was to continue for the nexttwenty years, our language.

To stipulate usage, when usage is outside the dictionary definition, is to add to clarity. And when stipulation will add to clarity and precision, we should never shrink from using it.

Descriptive Definitions

Unlike stipulative definitions, where the usage of a word in a narrow, precise sense is made explicit, *descriptive definitions* are the meanings attributed to words because of the ways in which they are generally used and understood. Descriptive definitions are the definitions found in dictionaries and lexicons. Descriptive definitions are the rules for the use of a word that are widely agreed upon. Descriptive definitions are bound by prior usage. Although a dictionary may provide a number of definitions for a single word, these definitions are given because of the varied ways and contexts in which the word is popularly used.

With descriptive definitions, context guides usage. Many words have many uses. Jonas Soltis uses the word "run" as an example of how context determines the appropriate descriptive definition. "Run" may refer to a fast race, what has happened to a stocking, the activities of a political candidate or a particular issue of floor covering in a carpet mill. "Run" may be used in yet other ways: run-of-the-mill, the river runs, and so on. Mortimer Adler makes the same essential point about the word love. There is romantic love, conjugal love, love of country, love of God, love of children, and so forth. Some languages, such as Greek, have multiple words for love, but this is not the case in English. Use of the word love, within a precise context, guides popular meaning.

C. A. Van Peursen, a biographer of Ludwig Wittgenstein, refers to the philosopher as having "an artistically sensitive nature," and as being "particularly nervous." "He walked sometimes with hasty, irregular steps" and would get "unusually excited" in discussion. Wittgenstein's personality, Peursen says, was "eccentric." All of the words used have multiple definitions in any dictionary. Yet the understanding of few if any people would likely falter because of the adjectives used. The author simply uses the words as he and the audience in general understand them and depends upon the sagacity of the reader to determine the precise meaning.

Use, however, may change over time. For example, theword "desuetude," to indicate "disuse," rarely occurs in modern English, particularly in the United States. The word can be found quite often, however, in scholarly works written earlier than the 20th century. Terms such as "liberal" and "conservative," as used in the United States following the 1988 presidential campaign, have meanings that are quite different from the definitions carried by the same words no longer ago than the 1960s. "Gay" is another example of a word whose use, and therefore meaning has changed within two decades. Until the 1960's, the preferred meaning of "gay" was happy, jolly, light-hearted, not homosexuality.

Occasionally we say that a statement is "simply descriptive," meaning the statement carries no hidden, extended or judgmental meaning. The speaker is saying that words are being used in the ways they are generally used, for the purposes of conveying messages that will generally be understood. Scheffler says, "if and only if the definitional equation purports to mirror predefinitional usage is it descriptive." We should assume a word is used to reflect what has been agreed upon as its meaning, unless the rules are deliberately and overtly changed. For instance, when George Boutwell, a 19th century governor of Massachusetts, secretary to the State Board of Education and later a United States senator, describes a public school as "a school established by the public - supported chiefly or entirely by the public, controlled by the public, and accessible to the public upon terms of equality, without special charge for tuition," he uses descriptive terms. His words are understandable, in earlier times and in the late 20th century.

Not infrequently, however, words are used in ways that are neither stipulative nor descriptive. For instance, when a word or expression is used to convey someone's agenda, the usage is likely programmatic.

Programmatic Definitions

Programmatic is the term Scheffler uses to identify definitions that convey a sense of *what ought to be (or what I want to be)* rather than what is currently the case. Programmatic definitions have a normative connotation, a moral dimension; they are "programmed" to convey a predetermined message, without being stipulative. A word defined programmatically focuses on a desired course of action or a desired end. Although a sense of the moral, and perhaps the emotional, are present the appeal of programmatic definitions is more likely to be cerebral than visceral.

Since ancient times, programmatic definitions have been a part of the reasoning process. In the *Ethics*, Aristotle says that even in the heyday of Greek learning different individuals and different groups defined terms in what today we might call programmatic terms: "For everybody agrees that justice in distribution should be based on merit of some sort; only people do not all understand the same thing by merit. Democrats take it to mean freedom, supporters of oligarchy wealth or noble blood and aristocrats excellence." Even Aristotle was not reluctant to use terms in the way he thought they *ought to be used.* "The origin of our friendly relations with our friends and the marks that characterize friendship seems to lie in our relations to ourselves. For a friend may be defined as one who wishes and does what is good, or what seems to be good, to another for that other's sake, or who wishes his friend to live and be safe for that friend's sake. This is the feeling of mothers for their children, and of friends, even if they have quarreled, for each other."

Americans have a penchant for defining words to fit what we wish to be the case. For example, writer Ann Lewis defines the modern-day push to restructure schools as the "renewal" of schools, perhaps reflecting a belief that an injection of new life is what is needed, not simply a reorganization.

Just as programmatic definitions can be stated positively and directly, they can also be stated either indirectly or deduced from what is said. For example, at the midway point of the 20th century, Adler said, "the broadest definition with which no one...can disagree is that education is a process which aims at the improvement or betterment of men themselves and in relation to society." To the contrary, many people can be found who believe that the sole purpose of education is the amassing of wealth and power, rather than the betterment of human beings.

Programmatic definitions can run the gamut of being obvious to being stealthily tucked away either in what is said or what is written. For instance, what the military wants and needs, Brauner and Burns argue, is order. By using the word conformity, the military is able to have more than order. The authors claim, "When men insist on more order than can be proven necessary, then they are asking for more than conformity." "Make no mistake," Brauner and Burns say, "conformity is merely a euphemism for a form of tyranny."

We can also ask questions programmatically. When Plato raises such questions as "what is justice?" and "what is courage?" he is not asking for definitions, but for how the terms are being used - what the two abstractions actually reflect, as used by the speaker. The context, the private or public intention of what the user intends, conveys the message.

Dr. Samuel Johnson, the 18th century English literary gadfly, uses and defines terms in his own, often humorous, way. Two of his definitions are exemplary:

Excise: A hateful tax levied upon commodities, and adjudged not by the common judges of property, but by wretches hired by those to whom the tax is paid.

Oats: A grain which in England is generally given to horses, but in Scotland supports the people.

Programmatic definitions can creep stealthily into negotiations which bear directly on the state of the world. For example, Churchill points out that in the 1930s, "Stalin wanted the Western nations to break off all relations with France and help the democratic forces in Spain to establish a regime agreeable to the Spanish people." The Russian ruler's use of the term "democratic," as cited by Churchill, and his view of what was agreeable to the Spanish people are suspect when measured against the common use of the expressions in the United States and Western Europe and the reality of life in countries controlled by communist regimes, both before and after World War II.

Finally, programmatic definitions can even be used to poke fun or debunk. In the first half of the 20th century, Robert Hutchins, then president of the University of Chicago and a major voice in attempts to reform higher education, defined a "university" as a collection of departments held together by a heating system.

To understand the functions of definition and use the concept appropriately is, however, only one vital part of communicating to which rapt attention should be given. The use of metaphors and slogans are also forever part of reasoning and communicating.

Metaphors

A metaphor is a means of comparison, using information with which the reader may already be familiar, to talk about one thing, with which the reader may not be familiar, as if it were something else. In a review of some of the historic efforts to restructure American public education, historian Michael Katz uses a metaphor: "For good reason the mass production of clocks and watches began at about the same time as the mass production of public schools." Thereafter, Katz indicates, both time and learning were governed by the stroke of the clock, by unswerving rituals which too frequently harden into rigid practices and expectations.

The use of metaphorical language as part of the reasoning process is both like and unlike reasoning by analogy. Analogies are used to reason because of the close similarities they have to the subject of discussion. Metaphors serve a similar function, but are usually stated in picturesque language. Analogies are direct comparisons; metaphors are implied comparisons. When the professor tells Jolene and Joann that they are "alike" because of characteristics one, two and three, which are common to both, then says, "but you are both as smart as a whip," he has used straight analogy, in the first comparison, and metaphor, in the second. Metaphors enhance our abilities to understand by pointing "to what are conceived to be significant parallels, analogies, similarities within the subject-matter of the discourse itself." Metaphors serve to lead students from the familiar to the unfamiliar, from the known to the unknown, from the routine to the poignant.

In English classes, students are taught to make a distinction between a metaphor and a simile. A simile directly expresses a comparison: A is *like* B; she runs like a deer. A metaphor calls something by a term which is not commonly used to describe whatever is being discussed; the comparison is implied. To call General Norman Schwarzkopf of Desert Storm fame, *Bear* is to use a metaphor. General Schwarzkopf clearly is not a bear, but when his soldiers and others call him Bear they are saying that in some significant ways he is like a bear, but without using the word "like."

In reasoning, however, the single term *metaphor* is used to include both "simile" and "metaphor." For example, in a book on the Middle East, Thomas Friedman makes a series of picturesque comparisons: "America [must learn] to play several different diplomatic roles simultaneously. She must learn to think like an obstetrician (do they want to get pregnant?), behave like a friend, bargain like a grocer, and fight like a real son-of-a-bitch." In the classroom Friedman's statements would normally be taught as similes; in logic they are treated as metaphors.

As is true of all comparisons, metaphors have limitations. It is a mistake to think of a metaphor as reality. Metaphors serve analytical and heuristic functions to bring a given concept into sharper focus, to enhance understanding. Metaphors stimulate thinking in new dimensions. Any analogy, any comparison, any metaphor, will break down at some point. No two things are exactly alike; if they are, then they are the same. When we use a metaphor, however, we deliberately assume the responsibility that the metaphor will clarify, not cloud, understanding. Given the vagaries of the English language, metaphors that clarify must be chosen with great care.

Perhaps no modern language exceeds English in being susceptibile to ambiguous, unclear usage. William Allen White, the longtime editor and publisher of the Emporia, Kansas, *Gazette*, and a counselor to early 20th century presidents, wrote a biography of President Calvin Coolidge which he titled, *A Puritan in Babylon*. The title is metaphorical and illustrates some of the teaching possibilities of metaphorical language. Literally speaking, President Coolidge was not a Puritan and Washington, D. C. would not qualify as Babylon. A moderately informed reader will, however, understand that White saw President Coolidge as a well-intentioned, perhaps somewhat naive man who as President was surrounded by people and circumstances of a lesser moral ilk.

In *From Beirut to Jerusalem* , Thomas Friedman effectively uses metaphor. Responding to questions about how the 1990s generation of Palestinians view PLO leader Yassir Arafat, a coed at the West Bank's

Bin Zeit University told Friedman, "Arafat is the stone we throw at the world." Literally, Yassir Arafat is not a stone, but figuratively (and perhaps prophetically) he is the most effective, if not the hardest, or perhaps the only, weapon the coed sees to accomplish the purposes of the Palestinian people.

Metaphors permeate our language and our thinking. "Gone with the wind," "the winter of our discontent," "small is beautiful," are all metaphors that have served as titles of well-known books. When Harriet Taylor, the love of his life, died, John Stuart Mill said the "spring of his life" was broken. Somehow, we understand more than if he had simply said, "my heart is broken."

Slogans

Slogans are different from definitions and metaphors, but have some characteristics of both. Not infrequently slogans are spawned by metaphors. Slogans are stylistic devices used to rally a cause, to get attention, to stimulate emotions, to send a message and sometimes todebunk or even destroy. When Winston Churchill asserted, at Westminster College in Fulton, Missouri in 1946, that "From Stettin in the Baltic to Trieste in the Adriatic, a great iron curtain has descended across the continent," he gave life to one of the great metaphors of modern times. The metaphor was to become a somber slogan. From the picture stimulated by the metaphor of an invisible (although from 1961 to 1989 the Berlin wall became visible) and impenetrable barrier marking off a great section of the eastern part of the European continent has come a slogan to define an historical period that lasted for more than four decades.

The "Iron Curtain" became a slogan to rally the Western world against the actions of an "evil empire," as once characterized by former President Ronald Reagan. Unintentionally, but in his ingenious way, Churchill gave the world a slogan to rally a cause, to stimulate emotions, to get attention, to send a message, to debunk and ultimately to destroy. "Iron Curtain" conjures up a part of the world and an era where people were restrained and stifled, where the sometimes faceless bureaucracy was amorphous, impenetrable and harsh.

Politicians use slogans frequently, with great purpose and effectiveness. Slogans get attention. For instance, every four years, citizens of the United States are called upon to rally to the support of one of several presidential candidates. More often than not the rallying cry is couched in the language of slogan. Franklin D. Roosevelt declared that "this generation of Americans has a rendezvous with destiny" and the nation listened. He captured the attention of the nation and of the world and gave life to a colorful metaphor that was to spawn a popular slogan - "rendezvous with destiny."

As it turned out, the rendezvous was to be "a new deal for all Americans," which became the "New Deal," Roosevelt's political, economic and social attempts to lift the U. S. out of the Great Depression. Americans were to understand that the New Deal was a program of action - the new administration would do what was needed to cause the economic and social conditions of the country to improve. The "old deal" was the result of a political party that was neither good nor fair for most Americans. The "old deal" was the result of the programs and policies of a group of privileged policy-makers out of touch with the mainstream of society. Historians are now about the task of assessing how well the generation of the time handled the problems of the time. There is little disagreement over the ability of the campaign strategists and policy makers to handle a phrase.

Slogans can fulfill an almost unlimited number of purposes. For instance, over time, slogans may come to be viewed as more literal than was originally intended. When people unwittingly fall into the trap of taking slogans literally expectations can be shattered resulting in bitterness and dysfunction. Most Americans living in the 1930s who literally believed that the New Deal was going to make life better for them were probably to some degree disappointed.

Slogans are sometimes employed in an attempt to convince ourselves and others that all is well with the world. When Prime Minister Neville Chamberlain proclaimed to the British people, and the world in 1938, "I bring you peace in our time," he uttered what was to become his epitaph in history. Hitler had already embarked on what was to be the most destructive, heart-rending, widespread war in history. "Peace in our time" is the slogan that will forever be associated with naivete, blindness, a lack of commitment and determination, the failure of will power and a lack of precision thinking.

In 1964, "All the way with LBJ," paved the way, in a landslide, to a full term in the White House for Lyndon Baines Johnson. In 1917 President Woodrow Wilson led the nation into World War I after vowing never to do so. It was, he said, "the war to end all wars" and "to make the world safe for democracy." When the young American nation wanted to justify its position over a boundary dispute, the slogan, "Fifty-four forty or fight," was spawned. When Republican presidential candidate and Speaker of the House, James G. Blaine of Maine, ran against Grover Cleveland in 1884 the bachelor Cleveland's amorous affair that had produced an illegitimate child was called into focus by the Republican cry, "Ma, ma! Where's my pa?" The confident Democrats retorted, "Gone to the White House, haw, haw, haw." And when young Americans rejected the moral grounds on which fighting men and women were sent to Vietnam, the rallying cry was, "Hell no, we won't go."

Just as politicians use slogans for their own aggrandizement, so do the scions of Madison Avenue. "We are bullish on America" is virtually empty of content. So is, "A tradition of Trust." Even the *New York Times'* slogan, "All the news that's fit to print" is open to question if taken as an empirical statement. But such statements are understandable and acceptable when viewed as slogans.

But how can clear thinking about some of the more obvious uses of language enhance teaching and contribute to a new pedagogy? Chapter 7 addresses that question.

Applications

1. Winston Churchill quotes Eleanor Roosevelt as saying:

> Mr. Vishinsky's assumption that all people who do not wish to return to the country of their origin because their countries are now under what is called a democratic form of government does not seem to allow for certain differences in the understanding of the word democracy. As he uses it, it would seem that democracy is synonymous with Soviet."

   a. On what problem does Mrs. Roosevelt's statement focus?

   b. Set up a logical argument that will reveal the error she exposes.

2. In an interview with a *Time* magazine reporter, the Russian novelist and political deportee, Aleksandr Solzhenitsyn, says that Lenin was "evil" because of "The absence of any mercy, the absence of any humanity in his approach to the people, masses, to anyone who did not follow him precisely."

   a. As Solzhenitsyn uses the word "evil," what kind of definition does he use?
   b. How can you demonstrate your answer by using a conditional statement?

3. In the 19th century, the British writer, Thomas Carlyle, argued that slavery was "natural." In rebuttal, John Stuart Mill points out that people seem to have a penchant for calling words, in this case "natural," whatever is to their advantage.

   a. If Carlyle called slavery "natural," then what kind of definition did he use?

   b. If Mill does not agree, then how does he reveal his disagreement?

c. Set up a Modus Ponens argument to demonstrate your answer.

4. Cardinal Newman is credited with defining a *gentleman* as "one who never inflicts pain."

    a. If Newman's definition is to be accepted, then what must support his claim?

    b. If Newman is saying this is the way a gentleman *ought* to act then what kind of definition is it?

5. During the 1988 presidential campaign, the term "liberal" was used extensively as a term of derision. Candidate George Bush of the Republican party constantly maintained that Michael Dukakis, the candidate of the Democratic party, was "liberal." Mr. Bush intended to convey the impression that Mr. Dukakis was out of the mainstream of American life. "Liberal" was being used differently from the way in which it is usually used in discussing the strands of life outside politics. The concepts of "to set free" or "generosity" were not the messages being sent to the American people.

    a. If Mr. Bush used the term "liberal" as he did, then is the definition descriptive, stipulative, or programmatic?

    b. If the definition is stipulative, then what makes it so? If not, why not?

6. Following publication of the his theory of evolution, Charles Darwin said, "The formation of different languages and of distinct species, and the proofs that both have been developed through a gradual process, are curiously the same."

    a. If Darwin's usage is an analogy, then is it a metaphor or a direct analogy or both?

    b. Rewrite Darwin's statement as a conditional statement.

7. Change each of the following slogans to a conditional statement:

    a. The truth will make you free.

    b. Arbeit macht frei (the Nazis' perverted use of the Biblical statement).

    c. Let my people go.

    d. We shall overcome.

    e. Duty, honor, country.

    f. "The great American road belongs to Buick."

    g. Veni, Vidi, Vici.

    h. Be prepared.

8. The poet, James Whitcomb Riley, supposedly once said, "The meanest man I ever saw, aw'ys stays within the law."

    a. If there is a reasoning problem posed by the statement, then what is the problem?

    b. Rewrite the statement to make it logical.

9. Emily Dickinson said, "Today makes every yesterday mean."

    a. If the statement is a reasoning mistake, then what is the mistake?

    b. Give an example of today making "yesterday mean."

10. Whitney says, "Doctors' offices are stuffy."

    a. If Whitney believes what she says, then what prior questions might help her understand her own reasoning?

    b. If Whitney is to clarify what she means by "stuffy" offices, then what must she do?

    c. Turn the statement into a conditional argument.

11. In *Their Finest Hour*, Winston Churchill calls the fleet of boats that rescued the allies from the breakers of Dunkirk as The Mosquito Armada."

    a. If Churchill wants his meaning to be clear, then what figure of speech does he use?

    b. Using conditional statements, explain Churchill's meaning.

See Appendix B for responses.

Chapter 7

Language And Learning

The mind of a people is expressed perhaps more immediately in the structure of its language than in anything else it makes....

H. D. Kitto

Words are always simpler than the brute reality from which they make patterns; if they weren't, discussion and collective action would both be impossible.

C. P. Snow

In the face of much successful teaching and learning, an unnumbered array of examples can be given of teachers who "present" well, but for some reason the desired learning does not take place. Sometimes students who want to learn go away either befuddled, having learned little or having learned the wrong lessons, or frustrated, believing they cannot learn. And sometimes students learn in spite of teaching. On the other hand, the failure of students to learn is not sufficient cause to conclude that teaching, in the sense of doing the "right things," did not occur. People learn in too many ways, under too many and varied circumstances to claim either that teaching is necessary to learning or that the presence or failure of teaching is sufficient to claim either success or failure in learning.

Teaching is guiding someone to know what was previously unknown. But the formula, **X** teaches **Y**, is not sufficient to claim that learning will occur. **X** must teach **Y**, **Z** - something. But even this formula is not a guarantee that teaching will result in learning in the fullest, richest sense. *X must teach Y, Z, so that Q.* Evidence that teaching has been effective is that the learner can act on what has been taught. If the purpose of a lesson is for students to learn that A + B = C, then the evidence that the teaching has led to learning is the ability of a student to make A + B = C *without the assistance of the teacher and then be able to use what is known.*

This chapter is an extension of chapter 6, with the emphasis on teaching. Examples of teaching and learning using definitions, metaphors and slogans are presented. In each case, the examples are developed within the context of the two reasons for the teaching of reasoning which were described in the chapter 1: to develop clear, precise thinking skills and to understand the nature of the knowledge.

Purpose: To Develop Clear, Precise Thinking Skills

In the American culture, a number of homey sayings are used to point out the level at which peoples' minds are perceived to function: "a mind like a steel trap;" "sharp as a razor;" "sharp as a tack;" or, conversely, "dumb as a door knob," "stupid as a fence post" and "a mind like a sieve." In every case, the expression indicates that the person in question has exhibited either a high or a low level of intellectual acuity.

A student's ability to take advantage of sound teaching is a combination of the intelligence brought to the learning situation, the environment in which the student is being or was reared, the education already experienced and the environment in which teaching takes place. Most people have either been deliberately taught how to reason or they have been able to figure out how to reason to some level of proficiency on their own. But whatever the cause, the number of people who can reason at a high, disciplined level is far fewer than should and can be the case.

A Case Study: From *A Separate Peace*

The discussion in the following sections is related to an excerpt from a well-known and frequently-taught novel, *A Separate Peace*, by John Knowles. In Knowles' story, following World War II, a young student, Gene Forrester, says:

Everyone has a moment in history which belongs particularly to him.
It is the moment when his emotions achieve their most powerful sway
over him, and afterward when you say to this person "the world today"
or "life" or "reality" he will assume that you mean this moment, even if
it is fifty years past. The world, through his unleashed emotions,
imprinted itself upon him, and he carries the stamp of that passing
moment forever. For me, this moment - four years is a moment in
history - was the war. The war was and is reality for me. I still
instinctively live and think in its atmosphere. These are some of its
characteristics: Franklin Delano Roosevelt is the President of the
United States, and he always has been. The other two eternal world
leaders are Winston Churchill and Josef Stalin. America is not, never
has been, and never will be what the songs and poems call it, a land of
plenty. Nylon, meat, gasoline, and steel are rare. There are too many
jobs and not enough workers. Money is very easy to earn but rather
hard to spend, because there isn't very much to buy. Trains are always
late and always crowded with "servicemen"....

Knowles provides examples of definitions, metaphors and slogans that
can add precision to thinking and to understanding.

Definitions

After saying that everyone has a "moment in history," the student
stipulates a definition of how he is using the expression: "It is the
moment when his emotions achieve their most powerful sway over
him....For me, this moment - four years is a moment in history - was
the war." By implication, he stipulates how the word "war" is used - it
is World War II. Knowles then adds to our understanding of his usage
by listing some of the characteristics of a moment in time. A moment
in time could be any moment, but Forrester means the years of World
War II. It's like saying "the game" and everyone understands that you
mean Ohio State vs. Michigan or Army vs. Navy or Rutgers vs.
Princeton. "Moment" is used in a programmatic sense to mean, "this is
what a moment in time means as I am using it." Whorf's contention
that language shapes perception is evident. The scene stimulates a
plethora of questions:

If the author reveals the national social atmosphere of the time, then
what was it?

If Forrester's experiences represent only those of a young man in a
preparatory school, then do they accurately represent the greater social
climate?

If Forrester is saying that what happened during the war years is indelibly stamped on his mind and personality, then will new realities not change them?

If we can find counter-examples within *A Separate Peace* to show that "a moment in time" is not universally accepted as four years, or as the years of World War II, then is Forrester's example of no use?

If the author *intends* to convey his views about a "moment in time," then are his views representative of normative standards of the time?

If Knowles says, " The trains are always late and always crowded with 'servicemen,' " then what, if anything, may he be revealing about his views of members of the armed forces?

If when Knowles defines "a land of plenty," then does he intend to communicate a sense of materialism that outweighs and over-awes all other definitions?

When Knowles has Forrester say , "Nylon, meat, gasoline, and steel there isn't very much to buy," then is he denying that the United States was "a land of plenty" during the years of World War II?

When the author has the main character define "moment in time," then is he revealing a tendency of youth to think in terms of the immediate, as opposed to a longer view and a more profound vision which bears on the larger parts of the story?

These questions can be turned into propositions, then into conditional statements, then into an argument for inquiry and examination:

> If a moment in history is experienced, then it is the four years of World War II.
> A moment in history is experienced.
> >A moment in history is the four years of World War II.

Or the argument can be structured to deny the consequent:

> If a moment in history is experienced, then it is the four years of World War II.
> It is not the four years of World War II.
> >A moment in history is not experienced.

Structured to either affirm the antecedent or deny the consequent, questions can be raised that lead to reasoning, investigation and understanding:

If the author defines a moment in history narrowly, then what is his purpose?

If Knowles intends to stipulate the definition of "a moment in history," then how can the reader know?

If a moment in history is not the years of World War II, then is there no "moment in history"?

If we think of a moment in history either as sixty seconds, or a "split second," or in any other term that conveys a sense of an instantaneous happening, then our thinking is conditioned to focus on the immediate. But Knowles collapses four years into a moment. Perhaps he sees the war years this way because the "world stood still" until the military fighting could be ended so that the issues between opposing political, social and moral ideologies could be settled. Is the author saying that nothing else could happen that was truly meaningful until the violence, the brutality of human and physical destruction which typifies war had passed? Are words used which appear to be descriptive, that is, used in the way they are used in everyday discourse, but which in fact are being used in either stipulative or programmatic senses? For example, how is the word "reality" used in the sentence, "The war was and is reality for me"?

Metaphors

Knowles uses a number of metaphors, some of them obvious, some of them more obscure. Consider, for example, the following statements by Forrester:

"...a moment in time";

"...he carries the stamp of that passing moment forever";

"The war was and is reality for me";

"Franklin Delano Roosevelt is President of the United States, and he always has been";

"...world stood still...";

"...split second...."; and

"land of plenty...."

Is each statement a metaphor? Does each statement enhance clarity and understanding? In each case, what does the metaphor represent? What is the message the author wants the reader to get from the use of each metaphor? How does each metaphor affect the scene in the story? If America is the land of plenty, then did anyone in the World War II era suffer from a lack of basic resources, as a direct result of the war? Change each metaphor into a proposition, then a conditional statement, then an argument, and discuss them with students.

Slogans

One of the slogans Knowles uses has long been both a blessing and curse in the United States -"a land of plenty." A number of questions can be raised to refine thinking and at the same time set students free to think in multiple ways about this story as well as other literature they read:

If the parochialism of Forrester restricts his view of the nation, then how does this parochicalism affect the story?

If statistics are available to demonstrate the wartime productive capacities of the nation in the economic areas listed, would the proposition change?

If the writings of other authors set in the same time with a cast ofsimilar characters were consulted would the same or parallel slogans likely be used?

A Case Study: From *Science for All Americans*

In this section, the subject matter changes from literature to science. In *Science For All Americans*, the American Association for the Advancement of Science introduces the chapter on the need to develop reasoning skills in students with the following statements:

...to the degree that schooling concerns itself with values and attitudes - a matter of great sensitivity in a society that prizes cultural diversity and individuality and is wary of ideology - it must take scientific values and attitudes into account when preparing young people for life beyond school.   Similarly, there are certain thinking skills associated with science, mathematics, and technology that young people need to develop during their school years.   These are mostly, but not exclusively, mathematical and logical skills that are essential tools for both formal and informal learning and for a lifetime of participation in society as a whole. Taken together, these values, attitudes, and skills can be thought of as habits of mind because they all relate directly to a person's outlook on knowledge and learning and ways of thinking and acting.

Definitions

When we consider that within the field of science in general, and the various specific areas of science, vocabularies have been developed that are unique to the subject matter and to scientists, the introductory statements to the chapter are written in clear, and understandable, everyday language. Even so, the language warrants further analysis.

A teacher can extend understanding of how words are used by examining definitions, which are rules for the use of words. Consider one of the terms the writer uses. Educators, the writer says, need to be "wary of ideology." The usage of "ideology" raises a number of questions and suggestions for examination.

When the term "ideology" is used, then what message is being conveyed?When the author uses "ideology," then to what is he contrasting it?

If the author is using "ideology" in a specific sense, then give an example of the term as he uses it.

If you can give an example, then give a counterexample, something that might initially be thought of as an example, but is in fact, the opposite of ideology.

If you can give both an example and a counterexample, then give the reasons that one is an example of ideology and the other is not.

Add a consequent to the following antecedent, then pursue whether or not the statement is true: "If society in the United States does not prize ideology, then...

Such questions can be examined by turning them into propositions, then conditional statements, then into arguments. For example, the question, "How is the term 'ideology' used? can be turned into a proposition:

The author uses the term *ideology* to mean a difference from how the American society is organized and operates, as opposed to some other societies.

Now the proposition can be turned into a conditional statement by asking the question, "To what is he contrasting *ideology*?"

If the author meant that Americans are wary of ideology, then the concept must mean a way of life that is different from the way the American society is organized and operates.

Finally, the question, "Why would a society such as the United States not prize ideology?" is addressed when the conditional statement is turned into an argument by adding a second premise and reaching a conclusion:

If Americans are wary of ideology, then it is because ideology means a way of life that is different from the way the American society is organized and operates, as opposed to some other societies.
<u>Americans are wary of ideology.</u>
>Ideology means a way of life that is different from the way the American society is organized and operates, as opposed to some other societies.

List some nations whose organization and government represent the concept of ideology. In what ways do they organize and operate that is different from a democratic government that is premised on ideals? How does the U.S. society use - and thereby define - "ideals"? What are some ways a society premised on an ideology might inhibit the pursuit of learning? What is *necessary* to an ideology? What would be *sufficient* for a society to revolve around an ideology?

The assertion that young people *need* to develop certain skills in school is a normative statement: This is the way it *should* be; this is the course of action that *should be pursued* in the education of youth. In defining what is intended by the expression,"certain" thinking skills," the author stipulates what is meant: the skills of mathematics and logic. Why would the author stipulate specific skills that students of science *ought to* have, then identify those skills as mathematics and logic? What specific skills of mathematics and logic are needed? What other intellectual skills may be needed? Is mathematics a skill in the same way that logic is a skill? Are these skills, combined with verbal skills, equally valuable either in other fields of study or in all areas of science?

At several points, the author uses the words "value" and "values" without stipulating what is meant. We may assume that the words are being used descriptively, therefore all readers will understand what is meant. But, in fact, the words are used programmatically. The author is referring to those parts of the American culture that are different - and by implication *better,* at least for citizens of the American nation - which should be preserved. As students engage in the study of science, they can also learn the nature of values, the basis for values, how to reconcile value conflicts, how to know when a presumed value is only a preference, and similar lessons.

Metaphors

At least two metaphors are used explicitly. First, the skills of mathematics and logic are identified as being essential tools for formal and informal learning and for living in the American society. The word "tools" conjures up a vision of an artifact with which work is done. In the context in which it is used, however, the word is a figure of speech used to reinforce the concept that both work, and therefore tools, are mental as well as physical. To work effectively and efficiently, students and citizens need to have proven, reliable intellectual tools. But with the tools of language and logic, students can examine their own and the thinking of others, as well as the language used. Language is a tool to convey thought.

A second metaphor is "habits of the mind." Close consideration of the statement stimulates a number of questions: What are habits? Does the author mean that a habit of the mind is the same as the habit of going to bed at 10:00 P. M., or eating corn flakes for breakfast, or taking a walk between 6:00 and 6:30? How broadly can *habits* be construed? What is the difference between a habit of the mind and any other habit? Is it possible to have a *habit* that is not at the same time a habit of the mind?

Slogans

Keeping in mind that slogans function to get attention, focus concern and arouse emotions that lead to actions, consider the author's use of the following slogans:

"cultural diversity;"

"thinking skills;" and

"habits of the mind."

As they are used, are the above slogans clear, unambiguous and useful? How do students understand the functions of slogans and how to separate the language of slogans from language used with a literal meaning? Consider an example. An expression frequently used earlier in the nation's history, which is occasionally still heard is, "the melting pot." In the last half of the 20th century the expression has been debunked in some quarters. The debunking argument goes like this: If the nation is a melting pot, then doesn't the claim imply that a melding occurs within the pot so that every part that comes out is unrecognizable from every other part? If so, why does the American society have informal, but real, social stratification? Why is there still discrimination, racism, sexism? Why are some groups more recognizable and therefore more separated from the mainstream of society than others? Why has it been more difficult for some groups to assimilate than it has been for others? If "melting pot" is valued by the nation's people, why is multi-culturalism being deliberately taught in the nation's schools?

In some quarters, the conclusions were and are that the expression - and therefore the slogans it has spawned - need to be changed. "Now we have cultural diversity" is a noble claim, but is it true, is it supportable? "Cultural diversity," just like a "melting pot" may be a desirable goal, but coining slogans neither creates reality nor resolves problems. Students can be helped to put slogans into proper perspective by the development of conditional statements and valid, logical arguments which at once stimulate their thinking and help in learning subject matter. For example, the slogan can be changed as follows:

If cultural diversity is a desirable goal, then the following steps must be taken to make the goal a reality (fill in the rest of the consequent):

1)
2)
3)

Students can be asked to supply the reasons, add a second premise, draw a conclusion then examine the argument for truth.

By using analogies, students can complete other learning activities such as the following:

Melting pot is to *(solution)* as *mixing bowl* is to *(suspension).*

Which metaphor more closely describes the United States? Is it important to change the metaphor?

When students understand the characteristics of a melting pot and the characteristics of cultural diversity, they are in a better position to determine which metaphor more closely resembles the reality of life in the United States.

Thinking skills and *habits of the mind* are separate slogans, but can be examined together. They can either be empty verbiage or provocative challenges that spur us to do something specific and concrete about the need to learn to think with clarity and precision. Students may be asked to write a list of the physical actions needed to develop the skills of throwing a baseball, then make a parallel list of the intellectual skills required to execute the physical skills. They might then make a list of the skills needed to be able to do long division, or multiplication, or subtraction or diagram a sentence. Which ones are physical skills? Which ones are intellectual skills? Can physical and intellectual skills be separated? Which ones are *knowing that* and which ones are *knowing how*? Are any both? Students may also discuss why they think a person, barring some kind of debilitating injury, never loses the skill of swimming or riding a bicycle. Is this true of every skill? If not, what is the explanation?

Purpose: To Understand the Nature of the Knowledge

From *The Birth of the United States, 1763-1816*

The following excerpt is from a history book by the late Isaac Asimov. It is written for students in the upper elementary and early middle school years.

As 1775 opened, Parliament had to consider the actions of the First Continental Congress and weigh the American reaction to the Coercive Acts. It was not as though voices were lacking to point out that it would be no use to continue with force; that in the long run the colonies could not be forced to accept a government they did not want; that it was wrong to try to make them do So. All foundered on the rock of the intransigeance of the King and his Prime Minister, Lord North. All Lord North would agree to do in the way of compromise was to offer not to tax any colony which turned over money voluntarily to the extent desired by Parliament. (To the colonies this was very much like having a bandit offer not to hold you up if you handed over your wallet voluntarily.) Even that much drew only a grudging consent from the King. Indeed, Lord North placed a new Coercive Act before Parliament on February 17, 1775. This would forbid the four New England colonies to trade with any nation but Great Britain and the British West Indies. New Englanders were not to trade with the other colonies and were not to make use of the Atlantic fisheries which were crucially important to the population. It was clear that Great Britain was

answering all appeals for relief by a further tightening of the screw so
the Massachusetts colonials continued to prepare for war.

Definitions

Although British laws restricting colonial commerce were called the
"Coercive Acts," Asimov assumes that students will understand the
expression. As Asimov uses the expression, Coercive Acts is
programmatic because it delineates what the Parliament thought *should
be* done, what course of action *ought* to be followed. And if widely used
in both countries to mean "force," then coercive is also used
descriptively.

Was coercion the term used in both the colonies and England? If so,
was it understood in the same way in each country? If the term was
either not used or not understood in the same way in both England and
the colonies, what explains the differences? Did the differences in
understanding affect the courses of action pursued by the British and the
colonists?

The sentence in which "coercive" is used the first time, qualifies as a
proposition. Several possibilities exist for the cultivation of reasoning
skills. For example, students can be asked to complete conditional
statements by adding a consequent to each antecedent:

If the acts were coercive, then Parliament expected the colonies
to_____.

If the British government named the acts, "Coercive," then they must
have wanted_____.

Asimov also uses the words *foundered* and *intransigeance* with an
apparent descriptive intent. He assumes the reader will know the
everyday use of the terms. What does *foundered* imply? Who
foundered? King George III, Lord North, the colonists? Is
intransigeance an intellectual or an emotional response? Is it both? Is
it neither?

Students may be asked to complete the following statements, add a
second premise and draw a conclusion:

1st. Premise: The Coercive Acts could be said to "founder" if and only if
_____.

2nd
Premise:_____.

Conclusion:
_____.

Draw (or have students draw) three circles, each inside the other. Have students label each circle either "British subjects" or "American colonists," or "intransigent British subjects." Have students explain why each circle is labeled as it is and placed in its particular relationship to the other circles.

Metaphors

To examine the metaphors used by Asimov, the first step is to change the statement to a proposition:

"Like having a bandit offer not to hold you up," is already a metaphor, stated as a proposition.

Second, change the proposition to a conditional statement:

If a bandit offers not to hold you up, then you may not know if he is a bandit.

Third, add a second premise and draw a conclusion to turn the conditional statement into an argument:

If a bandit offers not to hold you up, then you may not know if he is a bandit.
The bandit I met last night offered not to hold me up.
>I'm not sure he was a bandit.

Now have students make the application to the government of George III and its relationship to the American colonies.

Examination of a second perhaps less obvious metaphor can also be worthwhile:

It was not as though voices were lacking to point out that it would be no use to continue with force...

Questions about this metaphor can be pursued:

For the colonists to get a "fair shake," was it either necessary or sufficient for them to have "voices" in the British Parliament? Explain.

In the above question, what is the expression "fair shake" used to mean? If it was necessary for the colonies to have voices speaking in their behalf in the Parliament, was this sufficient for them to be "given a fair shake" by the British?   Using circles, diagram and explain the reasoning.

Slogans

The Coercive Acts gave rise to a slogan heard far and wide in the colonies and in Great Britain, a slogan that instilled fear in members of the British parliament. The slogan is not used by Asimov but fits into the discussion: *"Taxation without representation is tyranny."*

Why does this statement qualify as a slogan?

What purposes did the statement serve in the colonists' drive for independence?

As literally as you can, write what this slogan meant to the colonists? To the British?

How does understanding the use of this slogan help us better understand the Revolutionary Era of U. S. history?

Following his statement about the colonists not having voices in Parliament to speak on their behalf, Asimov says, "in the long run the colonies could not be forced to accept a government they did not want." Complete the following arguments, by adding a consequent to each antecedent, that either affirms the antecedent or denies the consequent, and reach a conclusion.

If the colonies were thousands of miles from England, then
_____.

If the British were so insensitive to the colonies as to pass the Coercive Acts, then_____.

Asimov uses another expression familiar as both a metaphor and a slogan: "tightening the screw." Complete the following statements and be prepared to discuss them:

If the British were "tightening the screw," then they were
_____.

If the screw was tightened, then the British could have expected the colonists to react by_____.

To further assist student understanding, questions such as the following may be asked:

If historians, such as Asimov, can write this story, then where do they get their information?

If they get it, then how do they get it?

If history is a "story," as often called, then what can be assumed about history?

If history is also an "argument," then what else can we assume?

If you can find any other of Asimov's arguments, then test them for validity and truth.

When the author says,"All Lord North would do...," then is he correct to use the word "all?" How can we find out?

When the author says, "Even that much drew only a grudging consent from the King," then what does he refer to as "Even that much?" Is thisthe whole story? What else could Asimov have told us that he did not include? Why might he not have told more? Does this usage indicate that history is "all of the past" or just that part of the past that historians have researched and reconstructed?

Applications

Included are some additional examples of statements from a variety of sources which may be used to teach either precision thinking or the nature of knowledge.

1. Referring to World War I, one biographer of Winston Churchill said: "In describing the enemy's practice of hiding in the hills and firing down at the moving British column, Churchill introduced his readers to a new word. Such a rifleman, he wrote, was 'a sniper,' as they were called in the Anglo-Indian army."

    a. If "sniper" was a "new" word, then where did Churchill get the word? How did he use it? How is the word used today? What would cause the word to mean either something else or another word to mean what *sniper* now means?

    b. Develop then defend an argument with the antecedent, "If Churchill coined a new word, then...

2. If higher education in America is frequently called "liberal education," then what is *necessary* to support the claim that students are provided a "liberal education?" Does such a claim meet the test of being *sufficient*?

3. If teachers of all subject matter present materials in biased, parochial ways - one point of view, one ideological perspective is tacitly presented in a more compelling way than are other points of view - then is such an education a "liberal education"? Set up an argument to examine and demonstrate your answer.

4. If some education is liberal, then some education must also be illiberal. Set up a Modus Tollens argument demonstrating what would be both necessary and sufficient to an illiberal education.

5. In chapter 6, the introduction to the *Declaration of Independence* is examined. If Jefferson intended his introductory statement as a programmatic rather than a descriptive statement, then how might our interpretation and use of the *Declaration* change?

6. What is the thought conveyed by each of the following metaphors?

   a. Some books are to be tasted, others to be swallowed, and some few to be chewed and digested.

   b. The New Deal, in fact, has been described as the life preserver that Roosevelt threw to capitalist America and that conservatives in their hatred of him and his program, threw back wrapped in epithets.

   c. The colonial experience is the tap root of American history the remainder of U. S. history is the nation's growing roots.

   d. "We have to handle this mating dance of gorillas that we're in carefully and one inning at a time. What are the metaphors and what is wrong with this statement?

7. Using the techniques of either Modus Ponens or Modus Tollens, examine the following metaphors and statements about metaphors:

   a. She used it to describe coming into Chicago on the train: "It's like seeing civilization with its pants down."

   b. Religions - all of them - are metaphors for the spiritual part of man.

   c. The idea of a machine is a metaphor for turning t he world into the image of man.

d. Myths are metaphors that refer to the transcendent.

e. History is a nightmare from which I'm trying to awake.

f. Weaving in new ideas.

g. Strike while the iron is hot.

h. Stream of consciousness.

i. Mathematics is a tool.

j. Tailor your lessons.

k. A family of words.

l. Getting through to students.

m. Information sinks in.

n. Do you see?

o. Hold that idea.

p. Beyond the scope.

q. Taming the west.

r. The roaring 20s.

s. King Cotton.

t. Third world.

u. Timeline.

v. Students are human resources.

w. The art of teaching.

x. Learning is grasping.

8. If each of the following statements is a slogan, then how can each be used to enhance the understanding of students?

   a. Nikita Khruschev's statement to a group of Los Angeles business men: "We will bury you."

b. The idea is to gather as much intelligence as possible on the competitors and then hit them with something *out of left field.*

c. We teach children.

9. Following Operation Desert Storm, in 1991, people worldwide became more acutely aware of the problems in the Middle East. Using conditional reasoning skills, examine the following slogans.

Some Arab slogans

a. Islam is the answer.

b. Enough is enough.

c. Never give up.

d. Mother of all battles (Saddam Hussein).

Some Israeli slogans

e. Stop the occupation (signs held by "women in black" throughout Israel).

f. There is a limit.

g. From Jordan to the sea.

h. Never again.

See Appendix B for responses.

Chapter 8

Informal Fallacies

The philosophy of reasoning, to be complete, ought to comprise the theory of bad as well as good reasoning.

John Stuart Mill

Frequently...the author of an argument uses a particular structure merely as a peg or diversion, while pressing his or her point home by a rather different route.

S. Morris Engel

An informal fallacy is a mistake that either distorts or shrouds the meaning of a statement. Informal fallacies have nothing to do with the logical form of a deductive argument. Mistakes, quite apart from the question of whether or not an argument is valid, are frequently made in the way language is used as well as in the reasoning process. Such mistakes are called informal fallacies.

Aristotle was the first person in Western civilization to group informal fallacies by type. He grouped them according to whether their genesis was in or outside the use of language. In all, however, Aristotle identified only thirteen different informal fallacies. The number and how they are grouped and labeled have expanded prodigiously since Aristotle's initial effort. But whether due to language usage or intellectual confusion, informal fallacies are, and have always been, bad arguments.

Informal fallacies may be made either innocently and unwittingly, or they may be deliberate. Sometimes, in the hands of a master, informal fallacies are consciously used to achieve an end that is antithetical to precision reasoning. Cleverness sometimes results in bad arguments for the sake of achieving a goal unrelated to clear reasoning. For instance, there may appear to be a relationship between logic and electing a political candidate, or selling a product or winning the support of people when, in fact, there are no direct relationships. Fallacies may be related either to carelessness, to careful thinking, in an attempt to mislead, or to moral standards. Such mistakes are also frequently called "common" fallacies. They are *common* as opposed to *formal* and they are common to all people, in every walk of life. Informal fallacies reflect on the *content*, not just the *form* of the argument.

Precision reasoning entails being able to apply the skills of logic to the formation of arguments as well as having the skills to spot mistakes in either the substance of an argument, the form of an argument or the use of language. S. Morris Engel has pointed out three compelling reasons for students to be clear about what informal fallacies are and how to recognize them. He couches the reasons as questions:

"Is the reasoning in the argument valid?"

"Is what the argument asserts clear?"

"Are the facts in the argument correctly represented?

Other questions can be asked when an informal fallacy is suspected:

Are the presumptions upon which the argument rests justifiable?

Are there any ambiguous elements in the argument?

Are solid grounds advanced in support of the claim?

Are the grounds advanced in support of the claim directly relevant to the substance of the claim?

Are grounds advanced sufficient to justify the assertion in question or is more evidence needed?

Although scholars have identified an almost unlimited number of informal fallacies, the basic pattern for grouping has changed little since Aristotle. In this chapter informal mistakes are grouped as Fallacies of Ambiguity, Fallacies of Relevance, and Fallacies of Presumption.

Fallacies Of Ambiguity

Fallacies of ambiguity are mistakes in the use of language. The misuse of language does not necessarily reflect a mistake in reasoning, but it may. Language strongly influences reasoning. And if used without either constraint, control or correction the misuse of language may lead to conceptual errors. Mistakes can be found in every nook and cranny of society. In this section, examples of five frequently encountered Fallacies of Ambiguity are examined.

The Fallacy of Equivocation

Equivocation is the inconsistent use of a term. The mistake is when the term is used more than once in the same context, but the user shifts usage between two or more legitimate meanings without indicating that the usage has changed. The problem is more complicated than simply being vague. Vagueness may or may not be due to a language mistake. The mistake is when a *shift* in meaning occurs which results in confusion and misunderstanding. "Stand on that line and don't give me a line" is equivocal. "Line" is used twice in the same context, but the meanings are different. English speaking people frequently use the same word to convey a variety of meanings. Context determines use and therefore meaning.

It is possible to equivocate either deliberately or unintentionally. Usually we are little concerned about the humorist who entertains us through the obvious misuse of language. But the ordinary language used by the humorist is also used at the highest levels of deliberations, which have the potential for consequences far beyond the everyday discourse of most people. Engel has pointed out that the fallacy of equivocation can be found in formal as well as informal reasoning:

All power belongs to the people.
We are the people.
>Therefore, all power belongs to us.

As stated, the argument is deductive, categorical and valid. But there is an informal mistake in the equivocal use of the word *people*. Between the first and second premise, the use of the word shifts. That our form

of government is grounded in "the people" hardly implies that the
people who live in Bedrock have "all power."

Charles Wilson, onetime head of General Motors and a presidential
cabinet member in the Eisenhower administration, is purported to have
said, "The business of America is business." For many Americans,
"business" may directly have little to do with the practices of
manufacturing, and commerce. Wilson's usage (if indeed he said it) was
likely for a purpose other than to convince us that the economic well-
being of all Americans is grounded in the world of business.

Examples of the intentional use of equivocation to both inform and
entertain sometimes help us see how easy it is to slip into the use of
the fallacy. In *The Age of Wit: 1650-1750*, Judson Milburn
deliberately equivocates:

> The Lordship being informed that a Lady lately d ivorced would
> probably be married to the Earl of Upper O_____y, said that it is
> about t ime s he was Upper O_____y for she has been under
> O_____y long enough.

While such writing may be entertaining, it can also serve a serious
educational purpose. Milburn erred intentionally. On occasion,
however, serious writers fall into similar usage, quite unaware.

In his combined biography, *Eleanor and Franklin*, Joseph Lash
recounts Mrs. Roosevelt's remembrance of an incident in the post-
World War II period. As Lash quotes the former First Lady, it is clear
that she recognizes the fallacy of equivocation in a conversation with
Mr. Vishinsky of the U. S. S. R:

> I visited two camps near Frankfurt [she replied], where the majority of
> people had come from Estonia, Latvia, Lithuania. They did not want to
> return because their country no longer belonged to them. They did not
> appear to me to be fascists and Mr. Vishinsky's assumption that all
> people who do not wish to return to the country of their origin because
> their countries are now under what is called "a democratic form of
> government" does not seem to allow for certain differences in the
> understanding of the word democracy. As he uses it, it would seem that
> democracy is synonymous with Soviet.

Historically, most despotic regimes have used language ambiguously to
the advantage of the regime, and with considerable finesse.

We also use language in ways that are not equivocal, but neverthess
in ways that distort the intended meaning, in ways that cause listeners
to be unsure about the message.

The Fallacy of Amphiboly

Amphiboly is the Greek word for "both ways." It is the mistake of constructing statements, that may appear to be well constructed, but the meaning is unclear. The communication is capable of conveying at least two messages when only one is intended. For Example, in *How We Think*, John Dewey says: "An earlier writer than Mill, John Lock (1632-1704) brings out the importance of thought for life and the need of training so that its best and not its worst possibilities will be realized, in the following words..." Does Dewey say that Locke brings out the importance of thought for life and the need for training *in the following words* or does he say that Locke does *so that its best and not its worst possibilities will be realized...in the following words*? The problem is focused on the uncertainty of what Dewey intends to be the antecedent of "it".

Because of the immediacy of the situation and the imperative to file news stories to meet a deadline, journalists are quite susceptible to the fallacy of amphiboly. For example, following a devastating loss of life at a human stampede prior to a 1989 soccer game in England, an American network news reporter stated, "In Britain, the police are responding to the tragedy of over one hundred people killed in an incident at the soccer game this morning." The statement raises the questions of whether the soccer game was played *this morning* or at some earlier time and was reported *this morning*, when the police responded. As the statement was made, it says that the soccer game was this morning. This is not just an example of a vague statement; it is a clear mistake. The soccer game had taken place the previous day. The following morning ("this morning" - the day it was being reported) the police were responding. But the time - "this morning" - cannot be dangled at the end of the sentence without distorting the intended message.

Examples of amphiboly are ubiquitous. For instance, Engel points out that the following two statements suffer because of the fallacy of amphiboly:

John and Bill ran a good race which he was gratified to win.

Clean and decent dancing, every night except Sunday. (A roadhouse sign).

One of the classic examples of amphiboly comes from the pen of Herodotus the "Father of History." According to Herodotus' story, the Greek king Croesus consulted with the Oracle at Delphi before making war on Persia. Responding to Croesus' inquiry as to the likely outcome, the Oracle said, "If Croesus went to war with Cyrus, he would destroy a mighty kingdom." Given such reassurance, Croesus felt secure in his aggression, attacked Cyrus and was soundly defeated. Beaten, confused and angry, Croesus complained to the Oracle. He was told that the prophecy was accurate. Croesus had destroyed a mighty kingdom - his own.

In the English-speaking world far too frequently clarity and precision are sacrificed because indefinite pronouns such as "this," "that," "it," "these" and "those," are used without a clear corresponding antecedent. As well as being a grammatical error, such usage can result in the mistake of amphiboly, which directly affects the clarity of communication. The carnival barker entices us: "Take a chance on a raffle for ten cents." Does it cost ten cents to purchase a chance, or is the pay-off ten cents? From the wording of the come-on, we cannot be sure. The barker has "amphibolied."

The Fallacy of Composition

The fallacy of composition is made when we assume that what is true of a part is also true of the whole. For example, to assume that because State University has eleven individually gifted football players the university will automatically have a great football team may be a mistake. By the time the team has been bamboozled in the fifth straight game, we may conclude that what is true of individual team members is not necessarily true of the team itself. By extension, we can look at almost any entity in the world and find the mistake. Four great individual singers do not necessarily make an outstanding quartet, and one hundred intelligent, skilled statesmen, do not, *ipso facto,* make a great deliberative body. *What is true of a part may not be true of the whole.*

The error crops up in all kinds of places, including the works of the most meticulous scholars. In *The Liberal Tradition in America,* Louis Hartz cites examples of people whom he calls "revolutionary thinkers" in America. From these examples, he then generalizes the concept of "some" revolutionary thinkers to "the Americans" - all Americans, a universal statement - as being revolutionary thinkers. Hartz cites two well-known characters in early American history, James Otis and Samuel Adams, as examples. The implication is that America has had a liberal orientation since its early history, that Otis and Adams were two such thinkers and that this liberal bent somehow fomented a liberal tradition in America. The tendency - the "tradition" - is historically accurate, but to attribute causality to Otis and Adams may be a mistake. A large gap exists between a few liberal-minded thinkers, some of whom may have been revolutionary thinkers in a time far different from the 20th century, and "the Americans" being revolutionary thinkers. We may not know how to judge when a person is a revolutionary thinker. What characteristics do revolutionary thinkers have in common? Or what do they have in common with people who are just "liberal thinkers"?

Finally, consider an example from William Manchester's biography of Sir Winston Churchill. Manchester points out that the historian "A. G. Gardiner had described the English Patrician as ' a personality that is entirely fearless,' belongs to 'a caste that never doubts itself.' " Winston Churchill may have been fearless and large numbers of individual English patricians may have been and may be fearless, but to reason that because such is true of some individuals the patricians are "a caste that never doubts itself" is a mistake. Gardiner was betrayed by the use of language. *What is true of a part may not be true of the whole.*

The Fallacy of Division

The fallacy of division is the converse of the fallacy of composition. The fallacy of division is to reason that what is true of the whole is also true of the parts. The fallacy is grounded in the use of language but can easily escalate into a mistake in reasoning. If we reason that because the school band has a great sound then every member of the band is an accomplished musician, we commit the fallacy of division. Such may or may not be the case. The fine sound of the band may be in spite of the indolent, haphazard third trumpet player.

If such a mistake was no more consequential than school bands, its commission would not be overly serious (although it's likely the band director wouldn't agree). Sometimes, however, both scholars and professional writers, as well as Everyman, make the mistake without being aware of the error. A *New York Times* writer of a widely read book on the Vietnam war says, "An American thinks of a road or trail as a line going from Point A to Point B, arriving only as necessary to accommodate terrain." "An American" may indeed think this way, but the context of the statement leads us to conclude that *all* Americans think this way. "An American," as the expression is used, is plural and universal. Of course, his conclusion could be empirically true, but that is not the point. Unless we empirically verify such an implication, which in such cases as this no one is likely to do, (no one is going to attempt to question *every* American on this point) then the proposition should be stated differently, in more precise language. The coincidence of being an American, or even an American soldier, does not dictate that one will view a line the way the writer claims. Some Americans may do so, and all Americans may have such a tendency. And it may not be the case that "all Americans" view much of anything the same way.

The frequency with which the fallacy of division is found in textbooks and works of scholarship is surprising. For instance, a one-time leading high school American history textbook says, "When England ruled its thirteen American colonies, the British government had passed laws to control business. The English wanted their colonies to help make England richer. They tried to make the colonies grow things needed in England, such as hemp, lumber and tobacco." The writers' use the expression, "they," "their," "The English," and "England" to delineate who were the instigators of the economic policies which resulted in widespread consternation in the American colonies and ultimately to war and a permanent change in the course of Western history. But the nation of England was composed of many hundreds of thousands of people of whom only a small percentage were responsible for the economic decisions relating to the colonies. Who were "they," or "them," or "The English," or "England"? Was "they" King George? Lord North? The House of Commons? The House of Lords? The judiciary? The barber, the baker, the candle stick maker? All of them collectively? Whoever the decision-makers were, it is a mistake to generalize from this amorphous group to the rank and file of English citizens.

Historian, Henry Steele Commager, in The *American Mind,* discusses the "American mind" which he says is "incurably optimistic," which "had never known defeat, grinding poverty or oppression." But can the characteristics of mind found in any grouping of people, however large or diverse, be construed as "the American mind"? To be sure, grinding poverty, oppression and debilitating pessimism have been experienced by many Americans. Or, is Commager referring only to decision-makers at the highest levels as "the American mind"? In truth, there is no "American mind." *What is true of the whole may not be true of a part.*

The Fallacy of Hypostatization

The fallacy of hypostatization is the mistake of treating abstract terms as if they are concrete objects. Sometimes writers and speakers border on giving abstractions humanlike qualities. In almost every case, we may easily say of the fallacy, "it is only the use of terms" and is, therefore, not of great consequence. We may argue that hypostatization enriches the language and adds vitality to concepts and discussions that otherwise become as dry as they are serious. To hypostatsize sometimes serves a purpose akin to the use of metaphors and slogans; usage enhances the capability to grasp elusive and difficult concepts and skills. In most instances the comparisons are clearly reasonable. But both students and teachers need to be aware that hypostatization is a verbal device and when taken literally, it can be a verbal error that evolves into an intellectual mistake.

For example, what is redness? What is sophistication? What is ugliness? What is beauty? Or, as Reichenbach stated many years ago, We never see 'the blue,' but blue things; we never taste 'the bitter,' but bitter things. In everyday discourse, as well as in scholarly circles, such terms are used with ease. But what are they? What do they represent? A face may be either red or blue. A person may have virtue. And a landscape may be either ugly or beautiful. Apart from the concrete entities which they modify, the concepts are merely abstractions. The problem is not just in using the abstractions as if they are concrete entities, it is also in doing so without recognizing we are doing so.

The English language, as it is used, is filled with examples of the fallacy of hypostatization. How can we thoughtfully ask what "nature" wants? Or what "science" or "history" teach us? Or what the "state" believes or demands? These and other such expressions are in the daily lexicon of language that we use to communicate in a host of ways. "The world will no longer laugh" is an expression of fear. But what does it mean? Should we no longer use it? "The world," as used here, is too amorphous to grasp with clarity.

Before the Battle of Trafalgar, in October 1805, Lord Nelson reportedly gave his battle orders with the amended mandate: "England expects every man to do his duty." Precisely to who or what Nelson may have been alluding by the expression, "England," we cannot be sure. But that he expected every man to do his duty was likely quite clear at the time. In truth, however, some mothers, wives, sweethearts, fathers, brothers and sisters may have had the safety of their loved ones as a higher priority than "to do his duty." These fearful loved ones, too, were part of England. As a device to make a point, the expression works well; literally it has the capacity to skew or obscure meaning and lead to fuzzy rather than precision thinking.

Finally, Gilbert Ryle places the fallacy of hypostatization in practical perspective: "A foreigner visiting Oxford or Cambridge for the first time is shown a number of colleges, libraries, playing fields, museums, scientific departments and administrative offices. He then asks, "But where is the University? I have seen where the members of the Colleges live, where the Registrar works, where the scientists experiment and the rest. But I have not yet seen the University in which reside and work the members of your University."

It is obvious that "University," as used by Ryle, is an abstract term. As centers of organized learning, universities do not necessarily consist of bricks, mortar, departments, administration, tuition fees, heating systems, and so on. By hypostatsizing the concept, universities may be thought of as tangible, near to humanlike, institutions. Such thinking is little different from Socrates asking Crito to imagine what the "Laws of Athens" would say if "such Laws" were to appear in his cell for a discussion. Who are the "Laws of Athens"? Where is the university? Perhaps Socrates, Crito and Ryle understood. Hypostatization should be used with skill and care, to assure that communication is enhanced and reasoning is not handcuffed.

Fallacies Of Relevance

Fallacies of Relevance are conceptual or thinking errors. Specifically, they are mistakes in arriving at a conclusion that is not supported by the premises; the conclusion is not *relevant* to the premises which are offerred in its support. Without a critically trained eye, most of us can be subtly seduced into accepting an argument that may at first appear sound, when in fact it is either ill-conceived or nothing more than an attempt to play on emotions. Engel says of Fallacies of Relevance that "when feelings run high, almost anything will pass as an argument." It is not uncommon to hear this group of fallacies referred to as *Fallacies of Irrelevance*. Either way, the premises in the argument are irrelevant to the conclusion.

The Ad Hominem Fallacy

Literally translated, the Latin expression *ad hominem* is to argue "against the man." In this section, direct and indirect ad hominem are reviewed.

It is not surprising to hear someone discount an argument for no weightier reason than, "he doesn't know anything," or "you can't trust a_____," or "we all know about his parents," and so on. The mistake is not relegated to small-talk, either in the general store, the grocery store or across the backyard fence. *Ad hominem* has an appeal in both high and modest places and manifests itself in a variety of ways. One of the most blatant and frightening uses of personal attack was the inhumane attacks by Hitler's Nazi regime. Nazi policy-makers went so far as to flaunt the Theory of Relativity based on the fact that Albert Einstein, whose scientific accomplishments revolutionized modern thinking, was Jewish.

Ad hominem attacks that are directed to either individuals or groups because of circumstances, past or present, sometimes tend to be less vehement than current, direct abusive attacks. Usually we refer to such attacks as "circumstantial ad hominem." When John Davidson, a member of the British Parliament, says to Lord Irwin that "Winston's [Churchill] game, of course, has been obvious, as it always is. He is not the son of Randolph for nothing," the attempt to discredit is transparent. But it is not a direct attack on Winston. Davidson uses the circumstances of Churchill's parentage to imply that one bad apple begets another and Randolph Churchill was indeed a bad apple.

An often-used way to attack another person is with *abusive ad hominem.* Instances of such use are ubiquitous, often as current as the morning newspaper. An example from the 1964 presidential campaign illustrates the fallacy of abusive ad hominem. J. Evetts Haley, a Texas rancher and one-time university professor, wrote a campaign biography of Lyndon Baines Johnson, the 1964 Democratic candidate for President. From the title to the last page, the book is an exercise in abusive ad hominem. Haley employs vitriolic attacks and negative, damaging allegations and insinuations against President Johnson. An example from the narrative demonstrates Haley's mistake: "If Johnson really cherished individual rights, his final statement of principle would inevitably be that of the traditional and true liberal - that the principal function of government is the guarantee and protection of those rights against trespass by others and by government itself. Not so with Lyndon B. Johnson. Instead, he believes that 'the most dynamic' responsibility of government is 'the prevention of waste - waste of resources, waste of lives, a waste of opportunity...' "

Ad hominem can be used against individuals, religious sects, races, ethnic groups and even nations. Sometimes the use is so subtle, conceivably not even recognized by the user, that unintended prejudices and extreme points of view are perpetuated. The author's style may betray the mistake. For example, the authors of one American history textbook have written: "Jackson gave government jobs to his political friends. This began what we call the 'spoils system.' He hated the Indians, and forced many of them to move west of the Mississippi. He ended the strong national bank, and did much to help pet banks in the states. These banks lent money to men who bought and sold land in the West. This meant that not enough bank money was left for other needs." Will evidence completely corroborate these claims? In the statements, the *ad hominem* is for the most part implicit, but no less present. The spoils system, the questions of how to treat the Indians and the matter of the national bank were all important national concerns. The authors could have developed rational, empirical arguments as a method of evaluation and as a basis for decision-making. To either reject or accept Jackson's decisions based on innuendo and insinuation is a mistake. If President Jackson was guilty of pork-barreling and nepotism, if he was moved to action by his personal biases and hatreds, and if he made crucial decisions on the basis of his personal economic desires, he still deserves to have his actions examined carefully, objectively and rationally.

The Fallacy of Poisoning the Well

The fallacy of poisoning the well is typically neither used very subtly nor fair to the ones against whom it is used. In the Middle Ages, prejudice against the Jews in Europe often caused them to be the focus of blame for whatever maladies affected large numbers of the population. When a plague of some kind attacked a population, it was common practice to blame the Jews. They had "poisoned the well." The expression has maintained its essential usage, but now usually refers to abstractions rather than concrete activities.

"Poisoning the well" occurs when a direct and deliberate attempt is made to undermine the credibility of either an individual or a group. The intent is to place the targets of the attack in such a position that any attempt at defense will further exacerbate the allegation that has been made. For example, suppose before a fair and impartial investigation has been made, a school principal says to the superintendent of schools, in the presence of a student accused of a violation, "We all know he lies like a rug, but we will let him tell his version anyway." How can the student respond? The principal has already laid out the ground rules: the student may speak, even though what he is going to say has been prejudged to be untrue. The well has been poisoned.

In his biography of Churchill, William Manchester quotes from Sir Henry Wilson's diary: "So ends in practical disaster another of Winston's military attempts. Antwerp, Dardanelles, Demkin. His judgment is always at fault - he is hopeless when in power." How could Churchill effectively answer the accuser? The well had been poisoned.

When presidential candidate, Michael Dukakis was accused of being a liberal, in the 1988 U. S. presidential campaign, how could he answer the charge in any positive way? When he attempted to do so, his attempt was considered defensive, which in the minds of the accusers was indicative of the correctness of the charge. The "L" word was soundly and roundly castigated. But how was the word being used? Was it automatically "bad" to be a liberal? What do liberals believe and does that make them undesirable as political leaders? Have liberals had many - or any - positive effects on the United States? Often, after the well has been poisoned, there is no compelling need to deal with such involved questions. The allegation is sufficient to achieve the intended result.

The Fallacy of Appeal to Authority

Remembering that Fallacies of Relevance are mistakes that reflect the irrelevance of the premises offerred in support of a conclusion, the mistake of appealing to authority can be at once seductive and dysfunctional to crisp, precise thinking. Whether the appeal is made either unwittingly or with great deliberation, the expectation of the arguer is that the conclusion will be accepted as *fait accompli* because of the authority cited in support of it.

An argument from authority may be couched in a wide variety of contexts: resorting to unusual words and phrases in an attempt to make the argument sound authoritative; referencing "unimpeachable" sources; quoting or referring to endorsements from well-known, highly respected individuals; and by overwhelming the recipient of the argument with the length of the argument. Or the argument may be stated in a crisp, specific way, such as the use of mathematical or symbolic formulas. Appeal to authority is an attempt to support a conclusion with something other than a reasoned argument, grounded in evidence.

To appeal solely to authority as the grounding for an argument may be a mistake for a number of reasons. Frequently, the proffered authority figure is in fact an authority but in a field that has little to do with the field in which his authority is being used. For example, there is no reason to believe that Albert Einstein, was an authority on social matters. And why should we suppose that either Willie Mays or Mickey Mantle are authorities on the best razor blades to use, even though both were great baseball players? Even if an authority's expertise is in the field cited, authorities can be wrong; an endorsement alone is not sufficient grounding for acceptance of an argument. Sometimes equally competent authorities disagree. Authorities may either be misquoted or misinterpreted or their messages severely distorted when, in fact, no such endorsement was ever intended. The appeal to authority is made in an almost endless number of ways. "Fifty million Frenchmen can't be wrong." "The Bible says so." "Look it up in Funk & Wagnalls." Such statements beg the question of the grounds on which an argument is based.

The Fallacy of Anachronism

The fallacy of anachronism is the mistake of ascribing the attributes of one era to another. The fallacy may be seen when a scholar in one period turns his attention to an era in which he is not an expert. For instance, one newspaper columnist has said that the "older generation" tends to judge the level of quality of the American public schools "based on their remembrances of when they were in school. If ever there is a time for tongue-clucking by the older generation, it is during the annual ritual of national moaning about SAT scores." The allegation is that members of the older generation judge the merits of modern American education by the standards and practices of another generation - remembrances that may or may not reflect the reality of the time cited as evidence.

When a young Arthur M. Schlesinger, Jr.'s biography of the life and times of Andrew Jackson appeared in 1945, its publication was followed by some claims that Schlesinger had actually attributed the characteristics of the Age of Roosevelt to the Jacksonian era. Although the initial volume of his multi-volume work, *The Age of Roosevelt* was not to appear until 1957, by the 1940s when he wrote The *Age of Jackson* , he was already recognized for his expertise in the New Deal era.

Every age and every incident has a right to be judged on the criteria which define it in its own day. To make the mistake, without regard to evidence, is to clutter the story of the past and misdirect the prospects of the present and the future.

The Fallacy of Presentism

Presentism is the mistake of examining and evaluating another era in terms of *current* circumstances. Cautioning against indulgence of the fallacy, Lawrence J. R. Herson, a modern-day political scientist, says "In seeking to understand changes from the Old Order to the present, care must be taken not to exaggerate these changes using the perspectives of the present. "The fallacy of presentism is a direct use of the wrong premises to support what may turn out to be the wrong conclusion.

The mistake of presentism is sometimes seen in the serious works of modern scholars. For example, in *The Crisis of the Negro Intellectual*, Harold Cruse recalls the 1930s: "As I pointed out previously, the exploitative racial factors involved in jazz music posed a serious and complex socio-economic, plus cultural, challenge. It was, in fact, the truly *native* American touchstone on which the whole concept of cultural revolution could have hinged - had the creative intellectuals, both black and white, seen the implications and faced up to them in political fashion. But the Negro intellectuals did not take up this issue, develop it, and fight it out as *their* issue, *their* stake, *their* main platform and *their* specific demand for cultural revolution."

Cruse was writing in the mid-1960s attempting to assess the plight of the Negro intellectual three and four decades earlier. He is accurate to allege that Negro intellectuals in the 1920s and 1930s were done dastardly wrongs. But it is by no means clear that even intellectuals in the 1920s and 1930s could see either the significance of their actions at the time or alternative ways in which they may have reacted. In the 1920s and 1930s the Negro intellectual was inhibited by a fear of not just his art forms being stolen but with the fear that his or other Negroes' lives would be endangered as a result of his actions. The 1920s was a period of renewed hatred and prejudice. The brutal activity of the Ku Klux Klan and other hate groups was widespread. To live in Harlem at the time did not exempt a Negro from covert fears of intimidation and danger even though the actual acts of repression may have been geographically far removed from him. Negroes everywhere in America still knew "their place." To lapse into the use of presentism to explain the earlier era does not result in a clearer picture of the earlier time.

The Reductive Fallacy

To attempt to reduce complex issues to simple solutions is a common practice in the United States. For instance, parents argue that students will do better in school if teachers will simply get tougher. Teachers argue that students will do better if parents will be more responsible. Some parents and some teachers argue that basic to the quest for improved academic performance is the need to "teach" students self-esteem. Conservatives argue that the resolution of the welfare problem is to make lazy people work. During the Vietnam war, "hawks" argued that the war would end when the United States decided to unmercifully bomb North Vietnam. "Doves," took the reverse stance: love, good will, and a greater sense of globalism were key to the solution. While bigness, complexity, bureaucracy, detachment, and the impersonalization of life are all manifested in many ways, problems that have historically been complex have rarely been amenable to one-dimensional solutions.

An academic example of the reductive fallacy can be seen in *The DuPonts of Delaware* by William H. A. Carr. According to Carr, Pierre Samuel DuPont, the first DuPont to permanently immigrate to America, played a central if not pivotal role in President Thomas Jefferson's negotiations for and purchase of the Louisiana Territory. DuPont, who was planning a trip to France in 1803, learned that Jefferson foresaw the likelihood of war with France if Napoleon placed French troops in the Louisiana Territory. According to Carr's account, DuPont suggested that the United States buy the territory to preclude problems with Napolean. In turn, Jefferson requested that DuPont combine official business with his personal trip to France. DuPont agreed and went to France to fill a diplomatic need as well as for pleasure. According to Carr, through the efforts of DuPont an arrangement was worked out for the U. S. to purchase the vast territory and a treaty was drawn up and signed. As Carr describes and explains what happened, a situation that had all the trappings of being a thorny international problem involving the grave questions of war and peace was settled amiably by the injection of Pierre Samuel DuPont into the diplomatic mix.

There seems to be no question but that DuPont played a role in the negotiations that led to the purchase of the Louisiana Territory. But that the procedures were as easily, smoothly and simply resolved as Carr presents them seems doubtful. The late Dumas Malone, one of the foremost 20th century authorities on the Jeffersonian era, sees DuPont's role as far less pivotal. Malone's description portrays the negotiations and purchase as a complicated diplomatic task. Everything Malone says about DuPont he says in relation to what took place prior to the actual treaty negotiations. In the chapter in which Malone describes the series of events and the actual treaty negotiations, DuPont is not even referred to by name. Carr's reduction of these complex negotiations clouds the reader's insight into the intricacies of international relations in the early 19th century.

Fallacies of Presumption

To presume is to think and act as if either facts or proof exist without knowing such to be the case. For example, George went to the airport without checking the flight schedule, presuming the flight would be on time. As a result George either had to return home and make a second trip to the airport or experience an unintended wait. In this section, some arguments that rest on unproven presumptions are examined.

The Fallacy of Sweeping Generalization

A sweeping generalization is the mistake of presuming that a generalization applies to all similar cases, without regard to extenuating circumstances. For example, while the declaration that all men are created equal is the lead assertion in The *Declaration of Independence,* to presume that the statement is irrevocably true in every conceivable circumstance is a mistake which can lead to other mistakes. In the United States, all people have equal rights and, we say, opportunities. Under the laws of "nature and nature's God," all men have equal worth. But to presume that the generalization of equality can be distributed to every circumstance in life, such as intellectual abilities, physical capabilities, and circumstances of birth is a mistake.

The fallacy of sweeping generalization sometimes appears in the most serious of debates. For instance, in the United States there is a long-standing difference of opinion over whether or not the government has the constitutional authority to pass legislation that controls citizens' rights to "keep and bear arms." The general right to do so is guaranteed by the second amendment to the Constitution. But can the general provision, as stated in the Constitution, be applied to everyone in every circumstance in modern times? Some prior questions help us grapple with the substantive question:

What did the writers of the Constitution mean by "keep and bear arms"?

Does the language in which the amendment was written in the 18 the century have the same meaning today?

Do either the circumstances of the 1770s or closely similar circumstances exist today?

Do circumstances exist today that may cause the amendment not to be generally applicable?

Is it possible to apply some restrictions to the second amendment without violating either the intent of the writers of the Constitution or the rights of modern U. S. citizens?

Generalizations are not laws in the same sense that laws exist in nature. A defining characteristic of a law is the absolute lack of exceptions. Exceptions to generalizations are, however, common. Fairness, even-handedness and prudence all dictate the need for careful examination rather than believing and applying a generalization irrespective of either the facts or their relevance. "Students don't want to learn," "all students are motivated to learn," "parents always act in the best interest of their children," and "every teacher enjoys teaching" are examples of sweeping generations that should be carefully examined before being accepted.

The Fallacy of Hasty Generalization

Hasty generalization can be a sweeping generalization with a twist. Decisions are sometimes made and actions are sometimes taken on the basis of a generalization that is reached too quickly; not because the circumstances on which the generalization is based do not apply, but because there are too few available facts at the time the decision is made. When Ginny sees her fiance having lunch with another woman, then generalizes (jumps to the conclusion) that he is not true to her, she may have made a hasty generalization. Because Sara's boyfriend was unfaithful, and the liaison with another woman began when he started having lunch with a female colleague does not guarantee that the same is happening in the case of Ginny's fiance. All the facts have to be gathered, then evaluated.

When a school authority, with no additional evidence, formally reprimands a teacher because one parent has complained that the teacher is not fair to students, the mistake of hasty generalization may have been made. It is a mistake to generalize that because one parent has complained, even if upon investigation the facts support the specific case, that all parents are dissatisfied.

To presume that because a suggestive movie was shown on television during prime time all commercial TV programs are "not fit to watch," is a hasty generalization. Specific information on each program is needed to support the claim. For Saddam Hussein to presume that coalition forces would not attack because they did not do so on the deadline date of January 15, 1991, may have been a hasty generalization. In everyday discourse, Everyman has long used the metaphoric expression "jumping the gun" to express the same idea.

The Fallacy of Bifurcation

The label for the fallacy of bifurcation is taken from two Latin words, which when combined indicate a concept is "two-pronged." The mistake is often recognizable by the dichotomous expression either/or. Bifurcation is to treat a *contrary* as if it is a *contradictory*. A contrary is two statements, or two situations represented by two statements, which cannot both be true, but both can be false. For example, when we say that Buford's complexion is either swarthy or ruddy, we have set up two alternatives that may be either true or false or that may both be false. Description of the texture and appearance of Buford's complexion is not restricted to two alternatives. We have set up a contrary when alternative conditions may prevail. On the other hand, a
contradictory exists when we say that Buford was born in either South Carolina or Kentucky. If one is true, the other is false, but both cannot be true. The fallacy of bifurcation exists when contraries, which leave room for other alternatives, are treated as contradictories, which leave no room for alternatives.

The mistake of treating contraries as contradictories - bifurcating - is made frequently enough to be a serious concern. "Either we spend more or the quality of education will deteriorate." "We cannot have strong education and good highways, too." "Education needs to go back to the basics." Neither the world in general, nor one segment of the world, such as education, is likely to be easily definable solely in inflexible, either/or terms.

The Fallacy of Begging the Question

Not infrequently a question is asked and answered presuming that a prior question has been asked and answered. The actual question is "begged" when the presumption is made that by reasserting the conclusion in another form, proof of the conclusion has been given.

When we argue that "A because of B" when A is the same as B we are begging the question. The reasoning is circular. The mistake can usually be avoided by use of a prior question. For example, to presume that Billy should not go to school today because he says the has a sore throat is begging the prior question, Does Billy have a sore throat? Or to argue that belief in an after-life is worldwide because "everybody believes it" is circular. Some prior questions are in order: Is there an after-life, and what is the basis for the claim? Prior questions get to actual questions and enable us to at least press for an appropriate answer.

When we have begged the question, we have offerred a tautology in support of an argument. For example, when we define "phonics" as the practice of sounding out words, we make a circular argument. "Phonics," as the word is generally used, means to learn the sounds of vowels, consonants and blends. Some prior questions, which will get to the question that is begging for clarification are, Why is the claim made that phonics is "the" way to teach students to read? Specifically, what is phonics? How is phonics used in teaching reading? Why in some quarters is phonics presumed to be superior to other methods?

The Fallacy of Begging the Question Epithets

Mistakes in the category of question begging epithets are related to the use of descriptive language; but they are more than language mistakes. These mistakes are conceptual errors that manifest themselves through the use of language. They divert attention from the question that needs to be addressed; the focus is on either peripheral or unrelated assertions. For example, suppose a senator says, "Judge Thomas lied to the committee and to the American people when he refused to state how he would vote on abortion." Use of the word "lied" diverts the focus from some prior questions: Was it a proper question for the senate committee to ask? Should Judge Thomas have directly answered the question? Emotions are aroused by use of the epithet "lied." The epithet skews the focus from the appropriate questions to what may only be side issues.

The question of whether or not Mr. O' Rourke can command the respect and direct the learning of students is brought into focus when the teacher enters the classroom and says, "All right, it's my time to put up with you dumbbells." The name calling, the insulting language, the sarcastic attitude which the language reflects, all beg the question of whether or not Mr. O'Rourke can teach and the students can learn. The actual question is obscured by a series of insulting epithets. Some prior questions are in order: Are the students dumb? Does this have anything to do with Mr. O' Rourke's professional and moral responsibilities? What is the first obligation of a teacher? What effect does the use of demeaning language have on the attitudes and capabilities of students?

Epithets that beg the question are often a resort to "mudslinging" and the use of "loaded words." At best, the use of epithets diverts attention from the serious questions involved in teaching and learning.

The Fallacy of the Complex Question

The complex question is a resort to what has ineloquently been called the "wife-beating" question. "Have you stopped beating your wife?" implies that the prior question, "Do you beat your wife?" has been asked and affirmed. The complex question entails the combining of two or more questions into what is intended to pass as a single question. The actual question frequently goes unaddressed, begging for identification. Questions such as the following all presume that a prior question has been asked and answered: How long have you been a bigot? Will we survive a nuclear war? What will senator X do after his defeat?

Even if apocryphal, the following story about Charles II of England (1660-1685) illustrates the fallacy of the complex question. The king purportedly asked members of the Royal Society to explain why a dead fish in a bowl made the water overflow while a live fish did not. After much embarrassment, uneasy discussion and conjecturing, one member suggested that they experiment to see if what the King implied by his question was true. When the hypothesis was tested it was discovered that whether the fish was alive or dead made no difference; the level of the water rose. Asking the prior question, Is there a difference? could have precluded debate and embarrassment.

In his review of Stanley Elkins' book on slavery, sociologist Nathan Glazer asks the question, "Why was American slavery the most awful the world has ever known?" The question begs the prior question, Was American slavery the most awful the world has ever known? Glazer's question cannot be answered appropriately until the prior question has been asked and answered. Both questions are empirical and can therefore be either confirmed or denied by evidence. To answer an initial question without answering a prior question may lead to confusion, frustration and perhaps miseducation.

The Fallacy of False Analogy

To reason by analogy is to employ a technique used widely, frequently, and profitably. Analogies can be used with great effectiveness to explain intricate, complex ideas or materials. But problems may arise when we either make comparisons that are not analogous or extend an analogy further than is reasonable and thereby lose the effectiveness of the comparison. The result can be one of distortion rather than clarification.

Analogies assume that when two events or objects have some similarities they will have other similarities. This is how we reason when we reason inductively. When used as an heuristic device to open up areas for investigation and gain new insights, reasoning by analogy can be useful and creative. But the technique can also be fraught with problems. False analogies can lead to the perpetuation of false information and ideas and can foster the development of flawed habits of the mind. Sometimes false analogies are the products of myth. For example, how many people still think Galileo's inspiration came from watching a pendulum swing, or that Sir Isaac Newton's inspiration came when an apple fell on his head?

The likelihood of using a false analogy may be reduced by paying attention to Engel's suggestion that when reasoning by analogy four criteria should be met:

The premises are true;
The degree of likeness is high;
The conclusion is not stronger than the premises can support; and
The conclusion is relevant to the premises.

An example familiar to most educators, enables us to focus on these four guidelines.

If third graders can go to the cafeteria unescorted by the teacher, just as fourth graders do, then they should be allowed to do so.
Third graders can go to the cafeteria, unescorted, just like fourth graders.
> They should be allowed to do so.

The premises are true, the degree of likeness - third graders vs. fourth graders - is high, the conclusion is supported by the premises and the conclusion is relevant to the premises.

Analogies should always be more familiar to the student than the material to be learned, should fit the occasion, and should not in any way distort the material to be learned.

Sometimes attempts at analogy are used in such a way that the strength of the analogy comes close to being the basis of the entire argument. The title of the late Crane Brinton's *Anatomy of Revolution* is an example. Brinton's purpose is to elucidate the concept of *revolution* by comparing the 17th century English Puritan revolution with the American and French revolutions of the 18th century and the Russian revolution of the 20th century. Analogies, however, stand or fall on their ability to demonstrate significant similarities. In this case, a title such as *Some Comparisons of Revolutions* may well have been more accurate. Violent revolutions do, in fact, have similarities. In the case of Brinton's "anatomy," however, the dissimilarities outweigh the similarities. The countries and times were different. The governments were different. The economies were different. And in the case of the English Revolution, violence was not used to achieve the end sought. The degrees of oppression were different. Brinton's analogies, and any analogy that fails to reveal significant similarities, should be used either with great care or not at all.

The Fallacy of False Cause

Sometimes referred to as *Post hoc ergo propter hoc* , the fallacy of false cause is the presumption that because one event happened before (or sometimes simultaneous with) another event, the one event caused the other. The problem of understanding and attributing causality correctly is the "chicken and egg" question that confronts everyone at some point. Causality is an abstract and elusive concept. Isaiah Berlin helps us gird for the difficulty of dealing with causality: "Our ignorance of how things happen is not due to some inherent inaccessibility of the first causes, only to their multiplicity, the smallness of the ultimate units, and our own inability to see and hear and remember and record and coordinate enough of the available material. Omniscience is in principle possible even to empirical beings, but, of course, in practice unattainable."

An example of the attribution of questionable causality is found in a statement from Joseph Lash's biography of Eleanor and Franklin Roosevelt. Referring to an incident during the 1920 presidential campaign, when Franklin Roosevelt was the vice presidential candidate on the Democratic ticket, Lash tells us, "Theodore Roosevelt, Jr., was dispatched by the Republicans to trail Franklin. 'He is a maverick,' young Theodore said in Sheridan, Wyoming. 'He does not have the brand of our family.' This personal attack galled Franklin, and it was the *beginning* of bad feelings between the Oyster Bay and the Hyde Park clans. " [Italics added.] The problem is Lash's attribution of the cause of bad feelings among members of the two Roosevelt families to the singular statement of young Theodore. The claim can be made that the remarks aggravated what was already at best a strained relationship. But to assume causality in such an absolute way, when the record reflects lingering bad feelings from earlier generations is to strain credulity.

Winston Churchill focused on the fallacy of false cause when he decried the widespread assumption that the Gold Standard caused poor economic conditions in Britain's coal industry in the 1920s: "The Gold Standard is no more responsible than is the Gulf Stream," Churchill said. Mortimer Adler claims, "Preschool deprivation is the cause of backwardness or failure in school." David Kearns and Denis Doyle argue that "Japanese students do so well on international comparisons because they go to school for a longer day than American students and a longer year." All of these statements may be partially correct. But they are also suspect when stated as the single cause of the events to which each is attributed.

Applications

1. Indicate whether each of the following statements is either a contradiction or a contrary then point out why this is the case.

   a. Chuck has a 4.0 cumulative GPA and undoubtedly will be chosen for the National Honor Society.

   b. If you are not with me, you are against me.

   c. All my beaux wear English Leather or they wear nothing at all.

   d. Susan is either happy or miserable.

   e. We must select either outcome based education or basic education as a usable model.

   f. School is hard work, not fun.

2. In the spring of 1992, the *Boston Globe* contained the following paragraph:

In what may prove to be his last major speech before leaving office, an emotional President Bush urged the United States on Tuesday to use its military force when necessary, but to do so in a highly selected manner.

a. If an informal mistake has been made that may distort the intended meaning, then what is the mistake?

b. If President Bush intended to urge the U. S. to be highly selective in the use of military force, then when did he make this statement?

3. In an article in the November 1992 *Atlantic Monthly*, Douglas L. Wilson inadvertently focused on an informal mistake in reasoning that can distort the modern view of Thomas Jefferson:

In accounting for Jefferson's behavior in the context of his own time, rather than ours, it is difficult for knowledgeable authorities to reconcile a liaison with [Sally] Hemings with much else that is known about him.

a. If an informal mistake has been made, then is Wilson pointing it out?

b. If the mistake distorts meaning, then how?

4. Identify the fallacy each of the following statements represents and give the reasons for your identification.

a. John and Lisa grew up together and married. The marriage will be happy.

b. Mrs. Jones' class received "happy" awards. Can we automatically assume that every student is happy?

c. When Erick asked how his Mom knew, she said, "A little bird told me."

d. I don't want you to play with Allison. Her Dad is a boozer.

e. They may appear to be fine people, but remember, they come from _____.

f. My Dad said so and my Dad knows.

g. Grandmother, were you allowed to watch TV when you were a kid?

h. All those people on public assistance should stop sponging and go to work.

i. All Frenchmen are Romantics.

j. Ahab is Arabic, therefore I know he hates Jews.

k. My mother cries; all women do.

l. Why am I the ugliest boy in school?

m. When is he going to do his own work and stop cheating?

n. Just like in the Roman Empire, and now it's happening here.

o. Pauline went wrong because she grew up poor.

See Appendix B for responses.

Chapter 9

Critical Thinking And Problem Solving

Imagination is more important than knowledge, for knowledge is limited, whereas imagination embraces the entire world - stimulating progress, giving birth to evolution.

Albert Einstein

The formulation of a problem is often more essential than its solution.

Albert Einstein

A problem well-defined is half answered.

Albert Einstein

It's better to debate an important issue without settling it than it is to settle it without debating.

Anonymous

Albert Einstein is the 20th century's quintessential metaphor for learning, erudition, creativity, academic pioneering, almost every kind of intellectual astuteness, and on a priority continuum Einstein ranks imagination ahead of knowledge. Einstein knew that absent imagination, the likelihood that knowledge will be used skillfully, wisely and productively is greatly reduced. Imagination, coupled with knowledge, skills, wisdom - and a requisite amount of humility - can enrich the context for solving the problems of life, including academic problems.

Creative thinking, critical thinking, and problem solving do not exist in isolation from each other. Problem solving entails reflection and calls upon our capabilities to think creatively and critically. Cognition and creativity are neither uncomplementary, antithetical nor separable. Well developed critical thinking skills require creative thinking and, in turn, creative thinking makes use of critical thinking to solve problems.

Decisions that need to be made are problems that need to be resolved. At some level everyone is constantly confronted with the need to make decisions. Making decisions and solving problems bring about change. What needs to change and what needs to remain the same are important considerations worthy of systematic reflection.

In this chapter, a distinction is made between *problems* and *puzzles*. In everyday discourse, problems and puzzles are often used as synonyms, but the concept of problems is a broader concept than puzzles. In problem solving, synthesis presupposes analysis. Solving a puzzle has the "right answer" as its goal and typically there is one way to do so. In problem-solving, using the skills of logic and analysis, the emphasis is on developing a *conceptual strategy* to frame a problem which, in turn, constitutes a context in which the problem can be examined and resolved. The intention is to provide a systematic, thoughtful way to initiate the resolution of problems, as opposed to an unerring formula. Critical thinking skills are tools to be used. To use reasoning skills to solve problems is to utilize analysis before reaching a synthesis.

Problem solving is not unlike learning subject matter; it's drawing inferences from the hypotheses we set up and the arguments we make. Problem solving is the *use* of knowledge. It's the ability to think analytically, to focus with precision and deliberation in order to answer a thorny question. It's *knowing how* by virtue of *knowing that*. Dewey saw all reasoning as problem-solving in the sense that it "is inquiry, investigation, turning over, probing or delving into, so as to find something new or to see what is already known in a different light." Dewey's view is the sense in which "problem" is used in this chapter.

Some Characteristics of Problem Solvers

The characteristics of problem solvers tell us something important about successful problem solving. Arthur Whimbey and Jack Lochhead contend that on balance effective problem solvers consistently exhibit five distinguishing characteristics:

1. *A positive attitude.* A confident problem-solver understands the skills he will use and how to use them.

2. *A concern for accuracy.* Accuracy is the result of precision thinking. Precision is the guideline that marks the path from where we are to the goal we seek.

3. *The ability to break the problem into smaller parts.* This task calls for the skills of analysis.

4. *Restraint to avoid guessing.* Guessing is not sufficient to resolve problems; at best the chances of success are contingent upon the laws of probability.

5. *A willingness to be active in the problem solving process.* To assume responsibility for solving a problem is at the same time to make the decision to confront the problem.

Anyone who sets out to solve a problem using the following, or any other problem-solving model, should first do a self-analysis to determine the personal attitudes and characteristics he or she brings to the problem.

A Problem Solving Model

There is no one right way to solve problems. We must approach problem solving by utilizing the skills and techniques we have learned elsewhere. A mathematician, a chemist, an artist and a novelist likely all have ways of resolving problems that are at once different from each other and different from their colleagues in the same field. For one, each has a peculiar and informed insight into problems specific to his area of expertise. Application of a systematic strategy will not directly produce "right" answers; it can, however, generate the "right" questions that will lead to appropriate solutions. In the remainder of this chapter, the following questions constitute a problem solving model:

1. *Can the problem be defined?**
2. *What do we want to achieve?*
3 *What do we know about the problem?*
4. *What don't we know that may be important?*
5. *What assumptions can we make?*

6. *Can the problem be divided into logical parts and which critical thinking skills can be used to solve each part?*

*As used in this model, "defined" means, Can the problem be placed into a class or category of problems, such as problems of language, practical problems?

Some problems are problems of language, others are problems of relationships and still others are problems related to either the instructional process, group dynamics or the developmental and maturational levels of students. Examination of some examples is instructive.

Problems of Language

Sample Problem

Mr. Talcler's high school literature class is studying Mark Twain's *Huckleberry Finn*. The following conversation between Huck and Jim stimulates considerable class discussion. Mr. Talcler sees the situation as an opportunity for students to learn some reasoning skills as well as learning the story of Huckleberry Finn. The following excerpt is from a conversation between Huck and Jim:

"Why, Huck, doan' de French people talk de same way we does?"
"No, Jim; you couldn't understand a word they said - not a single word."
"Well, now, I be ding-busted! How do dat come?"
"I don't know, but it's so. I got some of their jabber out of a book. S'pose a man was to come to you and say Polly-voo-franzy - what would you think?"
"I wouldn' think nuffn; I'd take en bust him over de head - dat is, if he warn't white...
"Shucks, it ain't calling you anything. It's only saying, do you know how to talk French?"
"Well, den, why couldn't he say it?"
"Why, he is a-saying it. That's a Frenchman's way of saying it."
"Well, it's a blame' ridicklous way, en I doan' want to hear no mo' 'bout it.
"Dey ain' no sense in it."
"Looky here, Jim; does a cat talk like we do?"
"No, a cat don't."
"Well, does a cow?"
"No, a cow don't nuther."
"Does a cat talk like a cow, or a cow talk like a cat?"
"No, dey don't."
"Well, does a cow?"
"No, a cow don't nuther."
"Does a cat talk like a cow, or a cow talk like a cat?"

"It's natural and right for'em to talk different from each other ain't it?
"Course."
"And ain't it natural and right for a cat and a cow to talk different from us?"
"Why mos' sholy it is."
"Well, then, why ain't it natural and right for a Frenchman to talk
different from us? You answer me that."
"Is a cat a man, Huck?"
"No."
"Well, den, dey ain't no sense in a cat talkin' like a man. Is a cow a man?
er is a cow a cat?"
"No, she ain't either of them."
"Well, den, she ain' got no business to talk like either one er the yuther of
'em. Is a Frenchman a man?"
"Yes."
"Well, den! Dad blame it, why doan' he talk like a man? You answer me
dat!
"I seed it warn't no use wasting words.... So I quit."

Analysis

1. Can the problem be defined?

The basic problem is one of misconception and misunderstanding
based in part upon both Huck and Jim's inadequate educational and
experiential backgrounds. Initially, however, the problem manifests
itself as a language problem. Jim does not understand that different
nationalities, and sometimes different cultures within a nation,
communicate in languages that may not be understandable to outsiders.
Even though there may be reason to suspect that Jim may understand
racial problems in ways that Huck doesn't understand, the language
problem must be dealt with first.

2. What do we want to achieve?

Huck thinks Jim is confused because he doesn't understand that a
Frenchman uses a language different from English. But Huck
temporarily gives up trying to clarify the point for Jim. In a real-life
situation, it would be important for us to overcome the misconceptions
Jim has about the use of a language with which he is unfamiliar as well
as his native language. Given Jim's understanding of the analogies
Huck uses, Huck may have mis-identified the problem. The unfamiliar
words and the physical differences between the way French is spoken
and the way Americans speak English compounds the problem.

3.   What do we know about the problem?

From the exchange between Jim and Huck, we can make a long list of factual statements:

Huck understands there is a difference between French and English.

Huck *may* have an insight into why Jim doesn't understand either the French language or the fact that all cultures and nationalities don't speak English, but he does not answer Jim directly. Instead, when Jim asks, "Why...doan' de French people talk de same way we does?" Huck replies, "That's a Frenchman's way of saying it."

Jim thinks the use of French is nonsense.

By asking if a cat talks "the way we do," Huck uses a metaphor to focus Jim's reasoning on something with which he is familiar.

By answering "No" to Huck's question, Jim reflects a degree of understanding.

Jim acknowledges that a cat ought not be expected to "talk" like a man.

Jim demonstrates a further degree of understanding by voluntarily extending the metaphor: neither a cat nor a cow ought to be expected to talk alike.

Huck confirms that he understands that a cat, a cow and a man are different.

In spite of what he understands, Jim continues to exhibit a restricted conception of the problem. He asks, "Is a Frenchman a man?" not understanding the ambiguous use of terms, such as "man."

When Huck confirms that a Frenchman is a man, Jim asks why, then, a Frenchman doesn't talk like a man.

In apparent frustration, Huck gives up on the grounds..."It warn't no use wasting words."

4.   What don't we know that may be important?

The problem is that Jim needs to understand that different nationalities and cultures sometimes speak different languages. In this case, we don't know - whether Jim and Huck have the same goal; whether the reason for Jim's initial question goes beyond the obvious, that he neither understands nor likes the use of French; whether Jim is curious about languages or simply irritated about the use of French - which he cannot comprehend - or simply wary of the unknown.

5.   What assumptions can be made?

We might ask the following prior question: Why did Twain write the dialogue between Jim and Huck? We can assume he did so to at least demonstrate a number of points: 1) the vagaries of language; 2) the thinking of people whose life experiences are restricted, provincial, and parochial; 3) the naturalness with which relatively unschooled but intelligent minds unwittingly deal with complex, esoteric problems; and 4) to reflect the rural, adolescent culture of the time.

6.   Can the problem be divided into logical parts and which critical thinking skills can be used to solve each part?

Usually, it is appropriate to make the most obvious divisions. The problem can be divided into the following parts:

Part #1: What Jim says.

Part #2: What Jim understands.

Part #3: What Jim doesn't understand.

Part #1:   What Jim says. To single out some specific statements for examination is useful. Jim's consternation over the use of the French language is reflected in a number of statements:

"ridicklous;"

"Doan' wanta hear it;"

"No sense in it;"

"No, cat's doan' talk like people;"

"Is a Frenchman a man?"

Jim's responses can be turned into propositions:

It is ridiculous to speak French when you could speak English.

I do not want to hear French spoken or a rationale for anyone doing so.

Cats do not talk the way people talk.

A Frenchman is not a man.

Each of these propositions can be turned into a conditional statement, then into an argument by adding a second premise and reaching a necessary conclusion:

If people can speak English [like a man talks], then it is ridiculous to speak French.
People can speak English.
> It is ridiculous to speak French.

If people can talk like a man [speak English], then I don't want to hear them speak French [nor do I want to hear a justification for them doing so].
People can speak like a man.
> I don't want to hear them speak French.

If cats talk like cats, then people should talk like people.
Cats talk like cats.
>People should talk like people.

If a Frenchman is a man, then he should talk like a man.
A Frenchman is a man.
> He should talk like a man.

By looking at the five arguments as a whole, it is apparent that Huck and Jim are dealing with more than just a language problem; it is also a conceptual problem. Jim does not understand the concept of "man" in the broad, generic sense. Life experiences have not provided Jim with the realization that other people are "men." He does not understand such a subtle concept as "mankind" and Huck is incapable of clarifying the point for him.

The first step is to consider "everyday" (descriptive) words that are either being spelled or pronounced differently from everyday usage. For example, clarity is served if we make sure that the following words are understandable:

"doan'" means don't;
"ridicklous" means ridiculous;
"en" means and;
"mo'" means more;
"Dey" means there;
"'em" means them;
"den" means then;

"er" means or;
"yuther" means other;
"dat" means that;
"seed" means saw; and
"warn't" means were not.

After examining words that are used descriptively it is important to determine if there are words that are used with either stipulative or programmatic definitions. In this example, there are no words used with stipulative definitions. But Twain uses the terms "argue" and "sense" in ways that suggest a programmatic usage. It seems more consistent with the story and the dialogue to view the usage of "argue" as more synonymous with "reason" than with disagree. For a lack of the intellectual tools to analyze the problem Huck gives up on Jim. For the lack of the skills of analysis, a useful synthesis cannot reached.

Part #2: **What Jim understands.** Jim understands there are some differences between animal species and the way each species communicates. This point reinforces the claim that what appears to be a language problem is at the same time a conceptual problem. Class reasoning is a suitable technique to lead students to understand both the language and the conceptual problem:

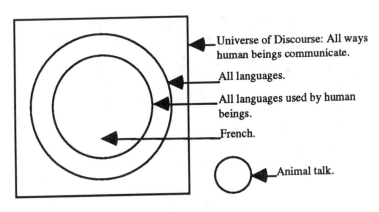

Figure 9.1

Since animal talk falls outside of the Universe of Discourse, further clarification can be achieved by examining animal talk as its own Universe of Discourse:

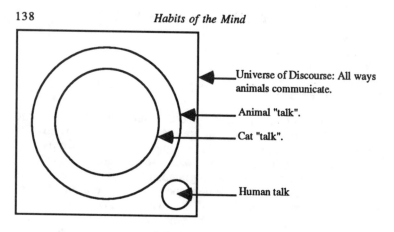

Figure 9.2

Human talk is not outside the domain of animal talk in the same way that animal talk is outside the domain of human talk:

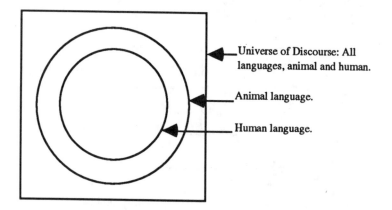

Figure 9.3

Given the empirical claim that some animals give evidence of understanding at least some human talk, we can demonstrate the phenomenon by the use of the diagram. Since there is little evidence to support the claim that human beings understand animal talk we will leave that point as being metaphysical and therefore unresolvable, and also as being unimportant to the solution of the problem we have identified.

Part #3: **What doesn't Jim understand?** Initially, Jim does not understand that animals communicate in ways that are unique to their species and that human beings communicate in ways peculiar to their various nationalities and cultures. We have already seen that he does not understand either the broad concept of mankind or the subordinate concepts of *nationality* and *culture.* Lack of understanding of these concepts is causally related to his inability to appreciate the use of a language other than English - which leads us to conclude that Huck's response, "Polly-voo franzy", was meaningless to Jim.

Since the goal of problem solving is to find and focus on a problem then isolate the parts of the problem to the extent that specific understandings can be developed, the task of teaching is to systematically guide the thinking of students to turn misunderstandings into understandings. The concepts of *necessary and sufficient* are useful tools. First, we need to create a clear proposition:

Jim does not understand the generic concept of *man.*

Second, we can turn the proposition into an argument by making it a conditional statement, adding a second premise and reaching a necessary conclusion:

If Jim does not understand the generic concept of "man," then he cannot understand that all men do not speak the language he speaks.
Jim does not understand the generic concept of *man.*
> Jim does not understand that all men do not speak the language he speaks.

Following the rule that the truth of the antecedent is sufficient for the truth of the consequent, we can conclude that Jim's lack of understanding of the generic concept of man is sufficient to guarantee that he does not understand that all people do not speak English. Then, following the rule that the truth of the consequent is necessary for the truth of the antecedent we can conclude that it is necessary to for Jim understand that all men do not speak English in order to understand the generic concept of man. Both the concepts of necessary and sufficient apply. We can then turn the statement into a biconditional:

Jim will understand the concept of multiple languages *if and only if* he understands the concept of man in its generic sense.

The term "man," as Jim uses it, is likely defined far too narrowly in his mind. His responses to Huck indicate that Jim thinks of man in the restricted sense of people whom he has known, possibly even in the sense of gender. If this assumption is accurate then without recognizing it Jim is using "man" in a programmatic sense.

Synthesis

Language problems come in a variety of formats. What appears to be a language problem may go far beyond language. Clarification of the language is of initial importance, however, since language is the medium in which the problem is expressed. After the problems are identified and placed in priority order, Jim's and Huck's problems are amenable to resolution.

Problems of Relationships

Solving a problem can be a significant challenge. For example, researchers working with business executives have discovered that when confronted with a problem that must be resolved, executives are more likely to be successful when the solution is either personally or professionally directly related to the executive. Teachers cannot avoid being directly involved in problems; but they must become part of the solution, not of the problem. In this section, problems of conceptual relationships, spatial relationships and problems of analogy are discussed. Some of the personal characteristics of teachers and the framing of problems for solution are briefly noted.

Problems of Conceptual Relationships

All problems are in a sense conceptual. The distinction is not between problems that are conceptual and those that are not, but between problems that are more concrete, on the one hand, and those that are more abstract, on the other.

Sample Problem

The following example focuses on the resolution of a global problem and the questions of war and peace. The problem is applicable to all students of all ages, provided the situation is presented on an appropriate level.

By 1990, President George Herbert Walker Bush had begun to speak about a "new world order" with some frequency. When in January, 1991, a coalition of armed forces from over twenty nations, led by the United States, launched a military attack on Saddam Hussein's forces both in Iraq and those occupying Kuwait, the President offered the need to establish a "new world order" as at least a partial rationale for the attack. Members of the legislature, the press, and the world community, began raising the question of what is a "new world order."

Analysis

To deal with the concept we need to have a common understanding of what is meant by "new world order." This understanding can be reached by applying the six-step model.

1. Can the problem be defined?

The expression "new world order" may be little more than a slogan. If the slogan is to become more than a catchy verbal device to get the attention of the world community, intense analysis directed toward some workable level of consensus is required.

2. What do we want to achieve?

It seems consistent with President Bush's motivation to interpret the phrase "new world order" as a desire to develop a scheme of global relationships that will lead to either the prevention or the peaceful resolution of conflicts. In part, the problem is one of definition. First, in the sense in which people understand the concept of war as a means to resolve problems, war is dysfunctional. A fighting war is barbaric and inhumane; in some ways, a cold war may also be. Wars are costly in every sense of the word: human life and well being, economic, materiel, spiritual, psychological and emotional. Second, the world needs an alternative to war as a means of resolving disagreements. Third, Mr. Bush should stipulate how he is using the expression "new world order" to enable other world leaders to address the same concepts. Definition will not solve the problem, but definition can bring the problem into sharp focus. Until the intention of the expression is clarified, and some common grounds for cooperative actions are agreed upon, "new world order" will remain a fuzzy, amorphous phrase.

3. What do we know?

We know at least the following facts: 1) Neither fighting nor cold wars have resolved disagreements without both sides suffering great losses; 2) mankind's capabilities to create and utilize weapons of human and material destruction appear to be virtually unlimited; and 3) following the Gulf War in the Middle East, there seems to be more receptivity to the concept of a new world order than ever before.

4. What don't we know that may be important?

Unless the leaders of the nations of the world are willing to say or
clearly demonstrate what motivates them to either seek or eschew a new
world order, there is no way to know who supports and who opposes
the concept. Which nations will participate? Will they participate in
good faith? Is democracy the worldwide wave of the future? What will
be the cost? How will the "new world order" function? The answers to
such questions are not apparent before the quest begins.

5.   What assumptions can be made?

We must assume that most of the nations of the world want a new
world order whose members will pursue the quest for democracy and
peace rather than resorting to totalitarianism and war. We must assume
the predominance of rationality over irrationality. And we must assume
that human beings everywhere have more commonalities than
differences.

**6.   Can the problem be divided into logical parts and
      which critical thinking skills can be used to solve
      each part?**

Given the existence of the United Nations, since 1945, we can
assume that Mr. Bush has in mind something that is either different
from or complementary to the United Nations. There is no reason to
assume that he is referring to a relationship of nations and peoples that
is divorced from - and therefore runs the risk of being antithetical to -
the existing world body. Based on this assumption we can divide the
problem into at least the following parts:

Part # 1:   Formulating a relationship between nations that does
              not resort to the use of war to resolve problems.

Part # 2:   Defining the functions of a new world order.

Part # 3:   Supporting a new world order.

Part #1:   **Democracy and the avoidance of war.**

First, we turn the statement into a proposition:

There needs to be a "new world order" to ensure a more widespread
adoption of democracy and an enduring peace.

Second, the proposition is converted to a conditional statement and then turned into an argument by adding a second premise and reaching a conclusion:

> If a democratic new world order is created, then the world will have more peace in more nations for longer periods.
> We do not have more peace in more nations for longer periods.
> > A new world order is not created.

The argument is valid, using Modus Tollens, denying the consequent. We can examine the argument further by using the concepts of *necessary* and *sufficient:*

> If a democratic new world order is created, the achievement will guarantee more peace in more nations for longer periods.

The most we can say with confidence is that a "new world order" *may be sufficient* for democracy and peace. But in order to have more democracy and peace in more nations for longer periods, it is not *necessary* to create a new world order. The same end may be achieved some other way.

Since the argument may meet the minimal standard of *sufficient*, but does not meet the standard of *necessary*, the power of the biconditional cannot be used. Depending upon how the "new world order" is defined, and how it functions, just the reverse can eventuate: war and mayhem may be required to achieve a new world order.

Part #2:   How the "new world order" will be defined and function.

If the new world order is defined as "working to achieve peace using only peaceful means," then war is obviated, at least by definition. If, however, the new order is defined as "working to achieve democracy and peace by whatever means are required," the desired outcome may have to be reached by means that are far from peaceful. If the "new world order" is designed and functions to supplement and give greater strength and credibility to the United Nations, will it function smoothly and well? If a new organization is created, completely external to the existing UN, can serious problems of commitment and allegiance be anticipated?

Part #3: Support for the new world order.

A new world order, however manifested, will need to have support, including moral and financial support. The point is cast into even sharper focus when a counter-example is created:

> If a worldwide democratic peace is needed, then the nations of the world must support a "new world order."
> <u>Worldwide democratic peace is needed.</u>
> >The nations of the world must support a new world order.

The use of a diagram can also help clarify the argument and its implications. For example, by the use of circles, students can see that the creation of a new world order can be sufficient to guarantee democracy and peace. But to have widespread democracy and long-lasting peace it is not necessary to have a new world order. In figure 9.4, where the circles overlap is the area where widespread peace is brought about by a new world order. In other areas, if there is widespread peace, it may be reached through means other than a new world order.

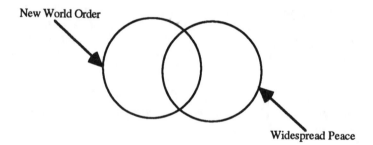

Figure 9.4

Should the argument be changed to reflect the goal of achieving more and longer periods of peace than are now the case, it could read as follows:

> If the world is to have a greater degree of long-lasting democracy and peace, then a "new world order" needs to be created.
> <u>A new world order is not created.</u>
> > The world is not to have a greater degree of long-lasting democracy and peace.

Diagrammed, the argument looks as follows:

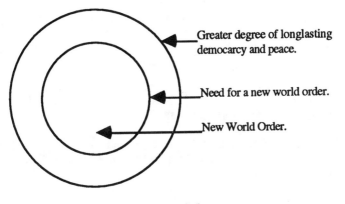

Greater degree of longlasting democarcy and peace.

Need for a new world order.

New World Order.

Figure 9.5

The original paragraph upon which this section is based can also be analyzed by turning the statements into a chain of reasoning:

1.0   If the President needed a rationale for the Gulf War, then the creation of a new world order was a reasonable choice.

1.1   If proposing a new world order was a rationale for entry into a war in the Gulf, then the war should have led to serious consideration of a new world order.

1.2   If the concept of a new world order was taken seriously, then the ideas expressed by the President in 1990 would likely be supported by subsequent presidents.

Synthesis

The concept of a "new world order" is at once so sweeping and complex that the creation of the machinery to achieve the goal is staggering. Until, however, the goals of the "new world order" are clear and acceptable by the majority of the world's nations and a practical relationship of a new order to the "old order" is believed to be achievable, the statement will likely be little more than a slogan.

Problems of Spatial Relationships

Spatial relationships are also conceptual relationships. It is useful to deal with spatial relationships as a separate category because they entail both physical and figurative space. Questions of physical space relationships frequently escalate into abstract questions.

Sample Problem

If X is standing beside Y and Z is standing beside X, then is Z standing beside Y?

Analysis

1.   Can the problem be defined?

The problem framed by the question is at once conceptual and abstract. We can, however, give the problem some concrete dimensions. Implicit in the question is the concept of closeness and we can assume that X, Y and Z are people.

2   What do we want to achieve?

Clarify the relative positions of X, Y and Z through a systematic, disciplined approach. When the names of people are substituted for the symbols, the problem takes on much more of a concrete representation: If Jane is standing beside Joe, and Peter is standing beside Jane, then is Peter standing beside Joe?

3.   What facts do we know?

Keeping in mind the characteristics of successful problem-solvers, one way to help students visualize the problem is to diagram the statement:

Peter (Z)   Jane (X)   Joe (Y)

It is obvious that Z is not standing beside Y.

4.   What don't we know that may be important?

We don't know either the context of the spatial relationship or the reasons for being together.

5.   What assumptions can be made?

We can assume that Peter, Jane and Joe are together for a reason and that for purposes of the current activity, their relative physical positions will not change.

6. **Can the problem be divided into logical parts and which critical thinking skills can be used to frame each part?**

The problem can be divided into parts:

Part #1: The abstract problem.

Part #2: The abstract problem that becomes concrete.

Part #3: Implications that may go beyond the immediate problem.

First, we can examine the problem by turning the proposition into a conditional statement:

If Jane is standing beside Joe and Peter is standing beside Jane, then Peter is not standing beside Joe.

By adding a second premise and reaching a conclusion, the conditional statement becomes an argument:

If Jane is standing beside Joe and Peter is standing beside Jane, then Peter is not standing beside Joe.
<u>Peter is standing beside Jane.</u>
>Peter is not standing beside Joe.

The problem can be used to confront other questions which are of educational value to students: Is Joe standing *too* close to Jane? How does society define *close* and *too close*? How are these lessons learned? What happens when we "violate someone else's space"?

Synthesis

This problem has several dimensions: The whimsical uncertainties of youthful behavior; the restricted capabilities to observe and gather information; and the need to use rationality. Unless the spatial relationship is analyzed with care and sensitivity, other problems, rather than a solution, may follow.

Problems of Analogy

Sample Problem

In *Problem Solving and Comprehension,* Arthur Whimbey and Jack Lockhead use the following sentence that requires a problem of analogy to be resolved:

_____is to plantation as car is to_____.

a. Kentucky: Detroit	b. tractor: passenger
c. agriculture: industry	d. tobacco: factory

Analysis

1. Can the problem be defined?

This is primarily a problem of analogy, understanding the use of language, specifically how words are used. Beyond how the key words are used, there do not appear to be any other language problems.

2. What do we want to achieve?

Reinforce logical, precision reasoning by analogy, which may be either abstract or concrete. The task is to use reason to make accurate associations. To do so requires an understanding of the concrete objects to which the words apply and the mental establishment of some characteristics that make two objects - and the two words that name the objects - appropriate analogies.

3. What do we know?

We know only the four groupings of words and that, based on *some* criteria or characteristics, we are to identify at least one of them as analogous to the statement, _____is to plantation as car is to_____.

4. What don't we know that may be important?

We don't know the criteria that identify the pairs of words as being analogous to the statement they are to match. And we are not told the educational value of making such associations.

5.   What assumptions can be made?

We can assume there is a legitimate relationship between at least one of the analogies and that the characteristics which legitimize these relationships can be identified.

6.   Can the problem be divided into logical parts and which critical thinking skills can be used to solve each part?

The way the problem is designed, it is already divided into logical parts. We should begin by focusing initially on the pair of words (concepts) with which we are most familiar. To do so, the problem can be framed as a series of conditional statements:

If Kentucky is related to plantation, then car must be related to Detroit in the same way.

If tractor is related to plantation, then passenger must be related to car in the same way.

If agriculture is related to plantation, then industry must be related to car in the same way.

If tobacco is related to plantation, then factory must be related to car in the same way.

The conditional statements can be escalated to logical arguments:

If Kentucky is related to plantation, then Detroit must be related to car in the same way.
Detroit is not related to car in the same way that Kentucky is related to plantation.
> Answer a cannot be the correct.

When set up as a logical argument, it is obvious that neither b nor c can be the answer either. Answer d is the correct response:

If tobacco is related to plantation, then car must be related to factory in the same way.
Tobacco is related to plantation.
>Then car is related to factory in the same way as tobacco is related to plantation.

The teacher is now in a position   to expand understanding by raising a series of additional, related questions:

If d is the correct answer, then how are tobacco and car alike in the argument?

If we match analogous words and concepts, then what lessons do we learn?

Synthesis

To understand and use analogies, we must be able to assume some likeness between either concepts, ideas or things to which the comparison is being made. The appropriate likeness will be determined by the total context in which the problem occurs. By using skills from logic and analysis, we are able to identify both the incorrect and the correct responses.

Problems and Practical Tasks

It is unrealistic to assume that all problems in schools can and will be confined to academics and the classroom. Schools include hallways, cafeterias, playgrounds, gymnasiums, fields and many other places which are only tangentially related to direct teaching and learning. In these areas we also need what Descartes said is the world's most widespread commodity, common sense, as a context for applying a problem-solving strategy.

Sample Problem

Whitney, Erick and Erin are in Ms. Goodlin's third grade class. Standing side by side at the blackboard, in the order named, they are attempting to solve arithmetic problems. Suddenly, Erick starts crying and hits Whitney. Whitney then begins to cry and calls Erick a nerd. The situation is spontaneous and volatile and can have serious implications.

Analysis

1. Can the problem be defined?

The outburst and physical violence have revealed that a problem exists between some or all three of the students. The problem is serious enough to cause physical and verbal abuse, but the cause of the outburst has yet to identified.

2. What do we want to achieve?

The causes for the outburst, including the physical violence, must be isolated before the problems among the students can be resolved. Without knowing the specific information in the current case, from her experiences Ms. Goodlin knows that student frustration levels can sometimes be high and their problem solving skills low. She needs to examine what happened and at the same time help all the students learn how to resolve problems amicably, rationally and non-violently.

3. What do we know about the problem?

The identities of the students, their positions at the blackboard and the outburst witnessed by Ms. Goodlin and the class is all that is known. Any other evidence must be gathered.

4. What is not known that may be important?

Ms. Goodlin does not know if there has been prior trouble among the students and if so what may have been the nature of the trouble. She does not know either the home situation of the students or if there is a relationship of any kind between the families of the three students.

5. What assumptions can we make?

Aware that she neither observed nor overheard a cause for the outburst, Ms. Goodlin is in a position to ask a prior question, such as, What caused this outburst to occur? Ms. Goodlin can safely assume that in all likelihood the incident is related to earlier interactions among the three students. If she asks a further question, What caused it to happen now? she may also assume that Erick wants help; otherwise, he may well have been wiser to wait until after school to hit Whitney.

6. Can the problem be divided into logical parts and which critical thinking skills can be used to solve each part?

One reasonable way to begin is for Ms. Goodlin to ask some questions of herself about prior decisions: How did the three students wind up in the same group? Is there any evidence that the problem has been brewing for a long time? Is having permanent work groups a good idea? How can the matter be resolved and preserve the learning atmosphere in the classroom and the personal images of the students, in their own eyes and in the eyes of the other students? How can the students be properly disciplined so that a healthy lesson is learned?

Habits of the Mind

Based on these questions, she might then divide the problem into the following parts:

Part #1: What happened before the outburst.

Part #2: The outburst.

Part #3: What the classroom situation needs to be after the matter is settled.

The problem of gathering evidence is the most obvious and pressing. After determining who was where and what happened, several skills of reasoning can be used. What was said, and by whom, may well play an important part in framing the problem for resolution. And how students use words among themselves - words such as *nerd* - has to be given some priority. Several conditional statements can be generated, then examined as arguments:

If Whitney was standing beside Erick, then she could not have been standing beside Erin.

If Erin was standing beside Erick, then he could not have been standing beside Whitney.

If Erick reacted first, then perhaps it was because of something said or done by either Whitney or Erin.

If Whitney called Erick a nerd, then either quietly at the blackboard or beforehand, then she must have said or done something to provoke Whitney since no physical contact was observed before Erick hit Whitney.

If Erick hit Whitney, who was not standing beside Erin, then is it likely that Whitney did whatever it was that provoked Erick to cry and hit her?

Synthesis

Only through careful, dispassionate analysis is Ms Goodlin able to formulate clear plans to deal with the problem. Anger, force or authoritarianism would, in the long run, serve her and the students far less positively. Having control over critical thinking skills gives her the power to analyze and resolve the situation.

Since the early 1980s, when the National Assessment of Educational Progress said, "problem solving is the one area that demands urgent attention," there has been some, but not marked, improvement in students' problem solving skills. More is needed, not simply because the problems are there, but because students have the potential to acquire and use critical thinking skills to resolve them. In theory, all problems can be solved. But *we* may not be able to solve them all, and some of the solutions may not be acceptable. Sternberg argues that when confronted with a problem, creative students are much more likely to pose questions than they are to brainstorm for answers. "They recognize significant and substantial problems and choose to address them", he says. Learning the skills to think critically and approach life analytically may be one of the most important lessons teachers and students ever learn.

Applications

How can each of the following problems be structured so that a solution can be reached? Demonstrate the strategy and list the reasoning skills to be used.

1. Carlene, a first grade student, is happy, congenial and bright. But in everyday conversation she swears profusely, probably not realizing that her language is socially unacceptable. Other students are beginning to use the same language. As Carlene's teacher, you sense considerable pressure from the community and the administration to do something about her use of language.

2. A small group of parents charge that Mr. Baker discriminates against female students. No educator has reported having seen any indication that Mr. Baker is discriminatory, but some parents are becoming concerned. As the principal you must resolve the issue.

3. Every student in Ms. Jones' class has memorized the times tables, but as a class they score low on mathematics achievement tests. Ms. Jones has been told, in unequivocal terms, that her students scores must improve.

4. Your next door neighbor is 70 years old and retired. He is healthy and appears to be able to maintain a comfortable standard of living. Although you are friendly with him, your neighbor constantly reminds you that he will vote no on any tax issue that will give teachers a raise in salary. You feel a responsibility to change his thinking.

5. Many of your students use expressions such as, "the reason is because," "where it's at," and "there are less of us than there are of

them." You want to change habits without either seeming pedantic or unintentionally giving the use of everyday language a distorted importance in the minds of the students.

6. As a high school English teacher, you want students to learn some of the great literature American writers have produced. Only one or two students, out of a class of 25, seem interested. You need to change student attitudes without sacrificing your initial academic goals.

7. Tom, Dick, Harry and Joe have ordered three pizzas. If they share the pizzas equally, how much pizza does each boy get?*

*Based on an experiment at the The Ohio State University early in the decade of the 1980s.

See Appendix B for responses.

Chapter 10

Changing The Paradigm

We have reached the point where we cannot bear either our vices or the cure.

Livy

I have a dream...

Martin Luther King, Jr.

...the prospects for man are very high.

R. Buckminster Fuller

Educators and the society in which we work *must* bear the cure for America's educational ills. Buckminster Fuller and Martin Luther King raise the banners under which we can pursue the quest for a stronger society, including stronger public education: conceptualize the potential for human beings, dream the dream, formulate the program, do the work. Public education cannot be sacrificed on the altar where homage has been paid for too many years: adequate education for a small percentage of students, mediocrity for the most, the weakest of broth for the remainder. The future belongs to other generations, not to us.

Students of today, citizens and leaders of tomorrow, cannot function effectively, cannot lead the world if the education they receive in public schools is not educationally designed to exploit their full potentials. While memorizing information will continue to be important, the ability to analyze and use information must become paramount. Mastery of the skills to achieve the first goal will strengthen the skills to achieve the second. John Herman Randall's claim that we can be said to "know" only when we can state with precision what we know and why, is worthy of careful consideration.

There is likely no single panacea for America's public education problems. To "run in circles, yell and shout" will neither fix the problems, slow the erosion nor deter the inexorable future. Unless we are willing to reasonably examine our practices and choose a "new pedagogy," one that is rigorous and demanding, educational historians may not treat our era kindly. As the world confronts a new century, the time is ripe for true reform. Bureaucratic shuffling will not be sufficient. It never has been. Reform without change is deceit; change without improvement is delusion.

However unintentional, the educational bureaucracy continues to honor the dictum of the ancient thinker, Petronium: "We tend to meet any new situation by reorganizing, and a wonderful method it can be for creating the illusion of progress while producing confusion, inefficiency and demoralization." From Petronium to Mrs. Hamilton of Massachussetts to the present, thoughtful people outside the education establishment recognize that bureaucratic, superficial reforms, such as reorganizing only the administration, or the governance of schools, or how education is funded will not improve teaching and learning.

Those people who believe in the progress of civilization, in the potential of human beings, in the refinement that only a strong challenge can produce must be the leaders of the future. Many of the challenges will be new and in some cases startling. If the challenges are to be successfully met, then the will of today must energize the work of tomorrow.

Many wispy efforts have failed to answer the question of how to improve teaching and learning. Simply to make schools more affluent is not the answer. To drive education with a behemoth bureaucracy is not the answer. To either create or perpetuate false dichotomies, such as subject matter vs. process, is not the answer. To assume that "self-esteem" is to be taught and learned in the same way we teach subject matter is not the answer. To continue to train teachers and administrators who are not grounded in the academic disciplines and therefore not educated in the richest sense of the term is not the answer. To conduct teaching and learning as entertainment is not the answer. To assume that students, all of whom learn much in the same way Aristotle learned, can make quantum intellectual leaps and survive without an abundance of knowledge and finely tuned reasoning skills is not the answer. And to mask the problems and shortcomings of education under a mantel of euphemisms is not the answer.

Progress, to say nothing of survival, demands that the tendency toward anti-intellectualism among educators be overcome. Precision reasoning must be learned by *all* students. Theoretical plans for teaching, learning and the measuring of what is learned must be reconceptualized. Educators should use a vocabulary that is consistent with the greater academic community as well as within public education. More should be expected of what can be learned from the academic disciplines, and the relationships of the disciplines. Human potential, not artificial categorization, must guide our determinations of how to educate all students. By changing and strengthening the paradigm used to energize and guide education, the exhilaration that comes from intellectual fulfillment can be reborn and rekindled.

In a meticulously conceived and eloquently written book, a quarter of a century ago, Thomas Kuhn argues that sometimes progress does not result from simply standing on the shoulders of giants. Times and circumstances may call for a change in the paradigm through which processes are concepualized and implemented. Public education in the 1990s is a premiere example. Figure 10.1 shows two paradigms that guide schooling today. One group of educators believes subject matter should be the core of schooling. Reasoning skills become an add on, an after-thought, not unlike sports and clubs. Another group believes the *process of education* is what matters most. For this group subject matter is a tack on, also peripheral to the core of schooling.

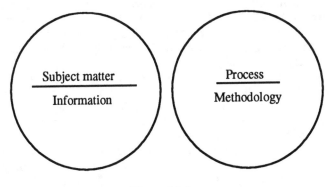

Figure 10.1

The paradigms for American education must be fundamentally changed. Reasoning must become an integral part of the teaching and learning of subject matter. Students aspiring to become teachers must master the skills of reasoning and become proficient in how to use these skills in all subject matter, at every level of learning. The paradigm can be simple and strong, as reflected in Figure 10.2.

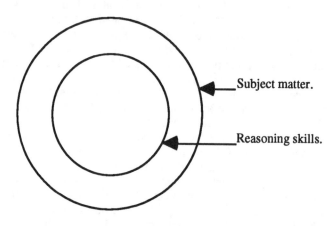

Subject matter.

Reasoning skills.

Figure 10.2

Such a model can effectively and efficiently deal with the unexamined assumptions that have guided American public education far too long. To teach reasoning as part of subject matter obviates any perceived need to assume that a given level of knowledge must be accumulated before a learner can begin to reason. *All learning*, not just memorization, "sharpens" the mind; but the mind can reason without *prior* sharpening. Implementation of a model that treats reasoning as an integral part of subject matter requires a teacher who is knowledgeable and skilled in the use of critical thinking skills.

Only when learning is structured to ensure that reasoning is taught as an integral part of the knowledge to be mastered and focuses specifically on precision thinking and the clarification and nature of the knowledge to be learned, will educators have a comprehensive model that serves as a copy to be followed, an ideal to be pursued and a standard for the measurement of progress. To begin the examination of subject matter with "if, then" is more precise, clearer and leads to understanding with far more consistency than to simply ask the ubiquitous "why?" If the answer to "why" is the greater goal learning should achieve, conditional reasoning is the method to reach the goal. To make explicit the content of the premises in an argument, including the use of language, the informal fallacies that may be present and the problems that may be implicit, is clearer than either unexamined generalizations, untested assertions or questionable conclusions. To understand the nature of the knowledge and the interrelationships of the academic disciplines reduces confusion and ambiguity. Students deserve this much. We must deliver the education they need. In the quest to know we must never surrender or lose sight of the common sense concept that analysis always precedes synthesis.

Appendices

Appendix A

A Student Learning Plan

A sample lesson plan which teachers prepare to guide student learning is provided to suggest ways to plan a lesson that includes the learning of reasoning skills as a part of subject matter.

Learning Outline

The following outline of a lesson plan is based on the chapter, "The Age of Monarchs," in *The Human Experience* (1985), Mounir Farah, Andrea Berena Karls, and Carl Max Kortepeter, Columbus, Ohio: Charles E. Merrill Publishing Company.

Prior Questions

Asking prior questions can add perspective to any lesson and should be asked.

1. Who are the students? *l0th graders.*

2. What is the subject matter? *World history.*

3. How will I find out what they already know about the subject? *Administer a pretest.*

4. What are the long-range goals? *Supplied by the teacher, based on the curriculum.*

5. What are the short-term objectives? *Supplied by the teacher, based on how the curriculum is arranged.*

6. What materials are to be used? *Textbook.*

7. In what formats will the materials be presented? *Reading, written activities, questions and answers, discussion.*

What will the teacher do?

1. Make the assignments, including the specific material to be read.

2. Provide explanations and clarifications. For example, the teacher may review the objectives of the lesson and explain and clarify the relationships between the lesson objectives and the course goals.

3. Provide learning activities to match student needs as determined by the pre-assessment of what each student already knows and the and goals objectives of the curriculum.

4. Conduct discussions, get the students intellectually involved, give cues, examples and guidance, provide feedback and correction, perform evaluations.

5. Convey a positive sense of satisfaction that comes from learning.

What will the students do?

1. Attend class.
2. Read the materials assigned.
3. Participate in class discussions.
4. Complete the exercises, activities and evaluations.

Every teacher may use the following examples of activities in a different way. For convenience and clarity, the activities are grouped under the reasons given for the simultaneous teaching of critical thinking and subject matter.

I. Purpose: To Develop Clear, Precise Thinking Skills

A. In the following exercises, write a conclusion to the first premise, write a second premise, then a conclusion to the argument that has been created. The first one is written as an example. The example is written to both affirm the antecedent and deny the consequent. In the exercises, complete the argument either one of the two ways, but at least one argument must be completed each way.

Examples

	If a king or queen wanted to control the nobility, then he
Modus	often gave them...[land].
Ponens	<u>Kings and queens wanted to control the nobility.</u>
	>Therefore, the king or queen often gave land to the nobility.

	If a king or queen wanted to control the nobility, then he
Modus	often gave them...[land].
Tollens	<u>Kings and queens did not give the nobility land</u>
	>Therefore, the king or queen did not control the nobility.

Exercises

1. If the monarch in England wanted to stay in power, then he (or she) had to learn to work with...
   (Second premise)
   >(Conclusion)

2. If Charles I of England had astutely assessed the religious problems of his father, then He would have known he could not stop the growth of...
   (Second premise)
   >(Conclusion)

3. Because Charles II understood why Charles I was executed, then he avoided irritating the...
   (Second premise)
   >(Conclusion)

4. Because Peter the Great believed progress in Russian society required opening the country to the West, then he...
   (Second premise)
   >Conclusion.

5. If the Russian peasants had not rebelled, Catherine the Great would have freed them anyway because she believed in...
   (Second premise)
   >(Conclusion)

Which conclusions are true synthetically? Which analytically? Which are metaphysical claims?

B. Based either on what you have learned, or what you believe is a reasonable response, complete each of the following statements. Be prepared to explain your statements.

Example

If the period 1500 to 1700 in European history is remembered as "The Age of Monarchs," then...we can assume that many European countries were governed by either a king or a queen.

Exercises

6. If Ferdinand of Aragon married Isabella of Castile and Castile came to dominate Spanish politics, then we can infer that Isabella...

7. If the defeat of the Spanish Armada by the English in 1688 symbolizes the beginning of Spain's decline, then it is reasonable to predict that the power of Philip II...

8. If Philip III and Philip IV lacked the abilities of their father and grandfather, Philip II, then we can surmise that when Philip II died...

9. If after the monarchy of Philip II the power of Spain declined, then the map of Europe was redrawn to show...

10. If after the deaths of monarchs who were decisive, aggressive, ambitious and ruthless, other leaders with such characteristics do not appear, then we may conclude...

Class Reasoning

C. Class reasoning techniques are sometimes useful to help students sort out confusing information. For example, the use of circles will quickly illustrate both that England was one nation ruled by a monarchy and who were the British monarchs of the 17th century:

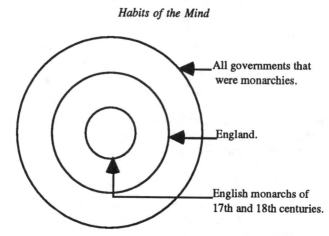

All governments that were monarchies.

England.

English monarchs of 17th and 18th centuries.

II. Purpose: To Understand the Nature of the Knowledge

A. One way to introduce students to the nature of the knowledge is to use statements by scholars in the field. For example, In *A Preface to History*, Carl G. Gustavson says:

> The historically-minded person knows that events do not occur in isolation; every happeningis brought about and conditioned by a series of events. He will, consequently, be impelled to seek for associations between the particular episode and others which may be connected with it. *In studying any present problem, idea, event, or institution, the mind of the historian inevitably gravitates in the direction of the past, seeking origins, relation-ships, and comparisons.*

Exercises

1. Use Professor Gustavson's paragraph to create a chain of reasoning.
    Begin by changing the proposition in the first sentence to a
    conditional statement then complete the reasoning chain. The
    proposition is provided for you. The historically-minded person
    knows that events do not occur in isolation.

2. Historians frequently are confronted with information from which they must draw a conclusion. To demonstrate this intellectual task, turn the following conditional statement (where the "if" and "then" are only implied) into a conditional argument, with a second premise and a conclusion, then be prepared to respond to the follow-up questions.

In order to understand how to improve Russia, Peter the Great had to understand what was happening in more progressive countries.
(Second Premise)
> (Conclusion)

Follow-up Questions

3. Create a conditional statement to answer each question. An example is provided.

Example

Q. Did Peter the Great deliberately set out to make Russia like the West?

A. If Peter the Great deliberately set out to make Russia like the West, then he insisted on Western styles of dress and behavior.

Exercises

Q. What did Peter mean by "improve"?

A.

Q. Does the statement say that to improve Russia it was *necessary* for Peter to know what was happening elsewhere?

A.

Q. Based on what the statement says, was it necessary for Peter to understand what was going on in more progressive countries in order to improve Russia?

A.

Q. Based on what you already know beyond the statement, or what you may find out, was knowing what was going on in other countries *sufficient* for Peter to improve Russia?

A.

D. Using quotations from the textbook will also help students understand the nature of the knowledge. For instance, have students change the following quotation into a conditional statement then respond to the follow-up quotations:

As a boy he [Peter the Great] had loved to play at war and had organized his friends into two military companies whose realistic maneuvers sometimes led to casualties.

Follow-up   Questions

What kinds of truth claims are being made?

How can you know that the claims are true?

What kind of reasoning do the authors use
to reach such conclusions?

Why do historians make statements such as
the above?

E. Complete the following biconditionals, then be prepared to explain your responses by offering reasoning and evidence to support your answers.

If and only if Peter understood what was happening in the West and took action could he expect..

We will understand the present if and only if we understand earlier...

Appendix B

Responses to Questions in the Applications Sections of the Chapters

Chapter 1

1. a. All three reasons can apply. To understand that the point in question is *either/or* is precision thinking. It can be both ways. The example can also be used to clarify fact from myth. Students can learn 1) how the myth of Washington chopping down the cherry tree began, 2) the role of myth in history and 3) how historical research does not support the Washington myth.

   b. Precision thinking and clarity apply to this statement. The former city of Istanbul is still there, but it is now called Constantinople. To know this fact, and to understand that the same city with a different name still exists helps students think clearly, particularly about change and historical evolution.

   c. All three reasons apply. That two plus two is four is an analytical statement. Precision thinking tells us this will always be the case regardless of time, setting or circumstances. That Benedict Arnold's actions benefited the British is true, based on current knowledge. But the conclusion is not irrevocable; it is based on the evidence available which is subject to change. For students to see how the math question can not change, but the history question may is to learn something of the nature of knowledge.

   d. This statement can relate to both precision thinking and clarity. Children follow a story so closely that if it changes at a second reading they are quick to point out the change. At the same time, stories are unparalleled tools to clarify some of life's complexities.

2. a. Assumption #1. b. Assumption #3. c. Assumption #2.
   d. Assumption #4.

Chapter 2

1. a. This is a synthetic claim. Whether the claim is true or false can be settled by evidence.

    b. "Spinster" is defined and used to mean an unmarried adult woman; therefore the claim is analytic even though it is a contradiction.

    c. Since the claim cannot be substantiated by either evidence or reasoning it is a metaphysical claim.

    d. Probably the claim is intended to be synthetic; as it is stated, it is analytic. A map of a states is a "picture" of the states.

    e. When the antecedent and consequent say the same thing the statement is analytic

    f. The statement is analytic. By definition"square" means a four-sided figure with equal interior angles.

    g. If Susan *says* she thinks Bill is handsome the statement is synthetic. But since we do not know whether she said what the statement alleges she thinks we have to treat it as metaphysical. We cannot, ipso facto, know what Susan thinks. She must tell us.

    h. Analytic. No amount of research will ever change this statement.

    i. "Heavens," when used to refer to space is a synthetic claim. But when we claim to know that God created the heavens the claim does not meet the standards to be synthetic and must be treated as metaphysical.

2. a. That b. That c. That d. That e. That f. Both. g. That h. Both i. Both j. Both.

Chapter 3

1. a. Your choice. Use the rules of inference.

b. Whether we begin with premises or gather and assemble information, an inference or conclusion must be reached. Therefore, in every case we reason "if, then..."

    a. Other examples:

        Armies are for purposes of fighting.
        Datum, not data, is singular.

2. b. Other examples:

        Phil ran the race.
        Team members ran the race.

3. a. Other examples:

        $10 + 10 = 20$.
        Girls + boys = human beings.

    b. Other examples:

        Lisa is teaching her children the value of high
        morals.

        Erin is getting a good education.

4. a. The claim states the evidence and therefore is synthetic.

    b. The claim cites evidence and therefore is synthetic.

    c. The claim presumes evidence and therefore is synthetic.

5. If you are unsure, reread the section on chain reasoning.

If work or a new style disturbed you, then it was probably good work.
If it is was good work, then...

6.   If people generally quarrel, then it is because
Modus   they cannot argue.
Ponens <u>They generally quarrel.</u>
        >They cannot argue.

Modus   If people generally quarrel, then it is because
             they cannot argue.
Tollens   <u>People can argue.</u>
             >They do not generally quarrel.

Chapter 4

1. However the marbles are sorted, students have to develop some criteria for making distinctions among them.

2. a. Whig. Over half a century after Washington.

    b. Fits. Believed in a strong central government.

    c. Fits. Led the colonial army in the Revolutionary War.

    d. Fits. First President of the United States.

3. Your choice.

Chapter 5

Since this chapter focuses exclusively on the use of the skill of logic to teach, no additional applications are provided.

Chapter 6

1. a. Mrs. Roosevelt focuses on the problem of definition, which in this case is a fallacy of equivocation. Mr. Vishinsky's use of the term "democratic" differs from the use in most of the Western world, so in that sense the term is equivocal. His use is programmatic; "democratic" is intended to mean something far different from how Mrs. Roosevelt used the term.

    b. If Mr. Vishinsky did not use "democratic" to refer to an open, free society then he used the term differently from how Mrs. Roosevelt used it.

<u>Mr. Vishinky did not use "democratic" to refer to an open, free society.</u>
>Mr. Vishinsky used the term "democratic" differently from Mrs. Roosevelt's usage.

2. a. Stipulative. Solzhenitsyn states how he is using the word.

    b. If Mr. Solzhenitsyn would stipulate his use of the term "evil",
       then he would eliminate misunderstanding.
       <u>Mr. Solzhenitsyn stipulates his use of the term.</u>
       >He eliminates misunderstanding.

Or, another approach can be used:

    This is how Mr. Solzhenitsyn uses the word "evil" when
referring to Lenin: absence of mercy, absence of humanity in his
approach to the masses or to anyone who did not follow him precisely.

3. a. Programmatic. Without saying so, Carlyle used the word
"natural" to mean what he wanted it to mean, but without stipulating
his meaning.

    b. Programmatic. Mill's accusation is almost direct.

    c. If Carlyle did not want to directly support slavery, then he would
      have used the term "natural" to his advantage to explain the practice.
      Carlyle did not want to directly support slavery.
      >He used the word to his advantage.

4. a. First, the use, therefore the definition, of the word *gentleman*
needs to be agreed upon. Second, since Newman uses the statement in
its universal sense - *all gentlemen* - one counterexample is sufficient to
discredit the claim.

    b. If Newman is implying "this is how a gentleman ought
to behave" then the statement is programmatic.

5. a. Mr. Bush uses the term programmatically.

    b. Although Mr. Bush may have strongly implied that Mr. Dukakis
was out of the mainstream of American life, he does not say so. The
definition is not stipulative because the use of word was not made
explicit.

6. a. Darwin's use is an analogy. There is no figure of speech. He
simply draws a comparison between different languages and species and
the concept of evolution.
    b. If different languages and distinct species have formed, then we
have proof that both developed through gradual processes that are
curiously the same.

7. a. If you know the truth, then the truth will make you free.

  b. If you work (arbeit), then you will be free (frei).

  c. If you let my people go, then you can be counted as a just person.

  d. If we persist, then we shall overcome.

  e. If you are a West Pointer, then you are expected to live by the credo, "Duty, honor, country."

  f. If I want to sell a specific automobile, then I may assert "The great American road belongs to Buick."

  g. If I came (Veni) and I saw (Vidi), then I conquered (Vici).

  h. If I am a Boy Scout, then my motto is "Be prepared."

8. a. Riley's statement is an empirical claim and therefore needs evidence to support it. The statement may also devolve into little more than a slogan.

  b. If an already mean man is careful to always stay within the law, then he is the meanest man I ever saw.

9. a. The statement is causal, therefore empirical. And as stated it presumes single causality - "Today." It comes close to an *ad hominem* since historians are the group who typically describe and explain yesterday.

  b. Frederick Lewis Allen's claim that the automobile became a house of prostitution on wheels in the 1920s qualifies.

10. a. Is this doctor's office stuffy? Are other doctors' offices stuffy? Are all doctor's offices stuffy?

  b. Stipulate how she is using the word "stuffy."

  c. If a doctor's office smells damp or smokey, then it is stuffy.
    This doctor's office smells damp and smokey.
    >This doctor's office is stuffy.

11. a. Metaphor. Churchill uses a figure of speech to imply a comparison.

b. Many small boats dotted the waters off Dunkirk, much as mosquitos sometimes dot the surface of a pool of water.

Chapter 7

1. a. Churchill introduced the term to the western world based on his earlier experiences in Africa. He used the word in a stipulative sense - for a single rifleman to pick out and shoot a single target. We use the word today in the same way Churchill used it. If, however, another word is widely used to mean the same as "sniper" the new term may supersede "sniper."

b. If Churchill coined a new word, then the word became widely used.
Churchill coined a new word.
>The word became widely used.

2. If American higher education is liberal education then a broad range of learning is included.
American higher education is liberal education.
>A broad range of learning is included in a liberal education.

3. If subject matter is not presented objectively, then the education is not "liberal."
Mr. Clio presents a slanted view of World War II.
>Mr. Clio's presentation of W. W. II does not constitute a "liberal" education.

4. If education is less than objective, then it is an illiberal education.
I am not receiving an illiberal education.
>I am receiving a liberal education.

When an education is in fact illiberal, it is necessary that the education be less than objective. When education is less than objective, this is sufficient cause to refer to it as "illiberal" education.

5. Programmatic usage would indicate that Jefferson was saying, *this is how it ought to be.* A case can be made for this point of view. Both scholarly and popular interpretation have, however, long held to the descriptive point of view. Jefferson is not just saying men *ought to be free*, rather he is describing what he already knew to be a fact in the colonies - *men are free.*

6. a. Based on the content and the purposes of the user, a book has more than one use. And every book may have a different appeal to different readers.

b. FDR saw his New Deal program as a way of saving the nation from drowning in poverty and despair. Conservatives, however, vilified the program with words because it violated their views of the Constitution and how the nation should be organized and governed.

c. Those decisions made in colonial times which led to the establishment, documentation and foundation of the American society did and continue to support the nation as it grows.

d. General Herres has mixed his metaphors. The activities of the Soviet Union at the time could aptly be labeled as a "mating dance of gorillas" and it was wise counsel to proceed carefully - "one inning at a time" - in dealing with the Soviets. To mix metaphors is, however, at best confusing and therefore defeats the purpose for using a metaphor.

7. These metaphors are for you. No examples are given.

8. a. Khruschev's statement in the late 1950s became a slogan. Literally it was a conditional assertion: If the U. S. and the U. S. S. R. continue on their current courses, then the U. S. S. R. will overcome the U. S.

b. This statement is both metaphorical and a slogan. Although the author saw "hit them with something *out of left field*" as a slogan, in fact, it is an apt metaphor meaning "they won't see it coming."

c. Of course we teach children, as opposed to walls or desks or even pets. So what does the slogan mean? Unfortunately, it has been used to either create or exacerbate the differences between "teaching children" and teaching children subject matter. The statement confuses the learner with what is to be learned.

9. These slogans are for you. No examples are given.

Chapter 8

1. All seven statements are contraries masquerading as contradictions.

2. a. This statement is an example of amphiboly, therefore his meaning is distorted and difficult to understand.

   b. Perhaps on Tuesday, but we cannot be sure whether the speech was on Tuesday or the president urged the use of military force on Tuesday.

3. a. The fallacy of presentism.

   b. By examining the events of Jefferson's time from the perspective of today's values and circumstances.

4. a. This claim is an example of hasty generalization. Growing up together and being acquainted do not automatically guarantee a happy marriage. More evidence is needed. The claim may appear to be synthetic. In fact, it is metaphysical. We can only speculate about what has not occurred.

   b. No. To do so would be the fallacy of division. We cannot assume that what is true of the whole is also true of the parts.

   c. Erick's Mom is indulging the fallacy of hypostatization. However she knew what she knew, she learned through human activity. Birds do not have the human characteristic of human speech.

   d. To shun Allison because of her Dad's habits is the fallacy of ad hominem.

   e. This statement is ad hominem. It also qualifies as the fallacy of poisoning the well.

   f. Dad may know plenty but to, *ipso facto*, assume he knows solely because he is Dad is the fallacy of reliance on authority.

g. There may have been no TV in grandmother's house. The question is either the fallacy of anachronism or the fallacy of presentism.

h. This statement is a sweeping generalization. What is alleged to be true of "all" may not be the case.

i. Sweeping generalization. Watch the "alls."

j. Hasty generalization. Ahab may not be Arabic and even if he is, being Arabic does not automatically make him a hater of Jews.

k. Another sweeping generalization.

l. Begs the question, Am I the ugliest boy in school?

m. First, the question begs the question, then the speaker resorts to begging the question epithet. The prior question is, Is he cheating? To call someone a name (cheater) without first determining that the allegation of cheating is true is a mistake in reasoning, as well as a mistake in human relations.

n. False analogy. To be perceived as a great empire in decline does not in itself make two situations analogous.

o. False cause. Many people grow up poor who do not "go wrong."

Chapter 9

This chapter is a series of examples. Use the strategy given to frame the problems for resolution.

Chapter 10

No application activities.

Glossary

Analytic: A statement is analytic if and only if the concept of the predicate is included in the concept of the subject.

Category: Kant says a category is a theory that does not have as its focus the elements of subject and predicate, but rather the whole statement. At one time "set" was used synonymously with category.

Class: A collection of entities of any kind that is typically specified by giving a condition for belonging to the class.

Conclusion: In induction, the most *reasonable* synthesis that can be reached, based on the evidence. In deduction, the *only* synthesis that can be reached, based on the relationship of the premises.

Conditional: A statement in which it is claimed that something either is or will be the case on the condition that some other condition prevails.

Contradiction: Two propositions so related that both cannot be true and both cannot be false.

Contrary: Either of two propositions so related that it is impossible for both to be true but possible for both to be false.

Critical thinking: Thinking that employs the techniques of analysis prior to reaching a synthesis.

Deduction: An argument in which it is impossible to assert the premises and to deny the conclusion without contradicting oneself.

Definition: A process or expression that provides the precise meaning of a word or phrase. A rule for the use of a word.

Fallacy: An argument involving an invalid rather than a valid form of reasoning.

Induction: A method of reasoning where an inference, or conclusion, is reached by observing and grouping particular facts or instances. From these facts an hypothesis is formed, stating what the facts mean, then tested against the facts for reasonableness.

Inference: A rule for the construction of an argument which says what may be inferred from one or more statements where logical structure is specified.

Informal fallacy: The expression often used loosely in general language to characterize any supposed error.

Knowledge: That which we can claim to know based on either evidence or the rules of logic. Knowing how, knowing that.

Logic: The study of the structure and principles of reasoning or sound argument.

Metaphor: A statement that makes an indirect comparison, points out a similarity, draws an analogy, often using picturesque language.

Metaphysical: An attempt to characterize existence or reality in its entirety. An attempt to explore the realm of the suprasensible, beyond the world of experience.

Modus Ponens: To affirm the antecedent in a conditional statement

Modus Tollens To deny the consequent in a conditional statement.

Premise: In an argument, one of the statements from which another statement (the conclusion) is deduced or of which the conclusion is presented as a consequence.

Problematic: A proposition that asserts that something is possible. Example: "It is possible that it will rain."

Synthetic: A statement (claim to know) that can be supported by evidence.

Slogan: A catchy statement designed to attract attention or stimulate emotions; such a statement is usually absent of substantive content.

Theory: A systematically related set of statements whose claims can be tested against evidence.

Truth: A property of propositions, singular statements. In popular usage, that which conforms to the evidence; agreement with reality.

Truth claim: An assertion that one has knowledge and grounds exist to support a claim to know.

Validity: A property of deductive arguments. When one premise follows another and the conclusion is necessary (no other conclusion can be reached), the argument is valid. When the rules of argument are followed, the argument is valid.

Select Bibliography

Action for Excellence: A comprehensive Plan to Improve Our Nation's Schools (1983, June), Education Commission of the States.

Adler, Mortimer J. (1990), Seven Philosophical Questions, New York: The Macmillan Company.

Adler, Mortimer J. (1982), *The Paideia Proposal: An Educational Manifesto*, New York: Macmillan Publishing Co., Inc.

Adler, Mortimer J. (1983), *Paideia Problems and Possibilities*, New York: Macmillan Publishing Company, Inc.

Adler, Mortimer J. (1988), *Reforming Education: The Opening of The American Mind*, Geraldine Van Doren (Ed.), New York: MacmillanPublishing Company.

Allman, William F. (1989), *Apprentices of Wonder: Reinventing the Mind*, New York: Bantam Doubleday Dell Pub. Co, Inc.

Anthony, Robert, (1979), *The Ultimate Secrets of Total Self-Confidence* New York: Berkley Books.

Arrendondo, Daisy E. and James H. (1990, February),Recognizing the Connections Between Thinking Skills and Mastery Learning, *Educational Leadership.*

Ayer, A. J. (1952), *Language, Truth and Logic*, New York: Dover Publications, Inc.

Ayer, A. J. (1955), *The Problem of Knowledge*, New York: St. Martin's Press, Inc.

Ayer, A. J. (1959), *Logical Positivism*, New York: The Free Press.

Ayer, A. J. (1984), *Philosophy in the Twentieth Century*, New York: Vintage Books, Random House.

Aylesworth, Thomas G. and Gerald M. Reagan (1969), *Teaching for Thinking*, Garden City, NY: Doubleday.

Axtell, James L. (Ed.) (1968), *The Educational Writings of John Locke*, Cambridge: Cambridge University Press.

Bailey, Stephen K. (1976), *The Purposes of Education*, Bloomington, IN: Phi Delta Kappa Foundation.

Bambrough, Renford (Ed.) (1963), *The Philosophy of Aristotle*, New York: New American Library.

Barell, John (1983, March), Reflections on Critical Thinking in Secondary Schools, *Educational Leadership*, pp. 45-49.

Beardsley, Monroe C. (1955), *Practical Logic*, Englewood Cliffs: Prentice-Hall, Inc.

Beyer, Barry K. (1990, February), What Philosophy Offers to the Teaching of Thinking, *Educational Leadership*.

Bishop, John H. (1992, March), Why U. S. Students Need Incentives to Learn, *Educational Leadership*, pp. 15-18.

Black, Max (1952), *Critical Thinking*, Englewood Cliffs, N. J: Prentice-Hall.

Black, Max (1956, spring), A Note on Philosophy of Education, *Harvard Educational Review*.

Bloom, Allan (1987), *The Closing of the American Mind: How Education Has Failed Democracy and Impoverished The Souls of Today's Students*, York: Simon and Schuster.

Bloom, Benjamin S. (1976), *Human Characteristics and School Learning*, New York: McGraw Hill.

Bloom, Benjamin S. (1981), *All Our Children Learning*, New York: McGraw-Hill Book Company.

Bloser, Philip 1990, fall), The A Priori In Phenomenology and The Legacy of Logical Empiricism, *Philosophy Today*.

Bolster, Arthur S., Jr. (1983, August), Toward a More Effective Model of Research on Teaching, *Harvard Educational Review*, pp. 294-308.

Boyer, Ernest (1990), *Scholarship Reconsidered*, Princeton, NJ: Carnegie Foundation for the Advancement of Teaching.

Brandt, Ron (1989, September), On Liberal Education for Tomorrow'sWorld: A Conversation with Douglas Heath, *Educational Leadership*.

Branford, John D. and Barry S. Stein (1984), *The Ideal Problem Solver*, New York: W. H. Freeman & Co.

Brauner, Charles J. and Hobert W. Burns (1965), *Problems in Education and Philosophy*, Englewood Cliffs: Prentice-Hall, Inc.

Brinton, Crane (1955), *Ideas and Men,* Englewood Cliffs: Prentice Hall.
Bronowski, J. and Bruce Mazlish (1975), *The Western I ntellectual Tradition: From Leonardo to Hegel,* New York:Harper & Row, Publishers.

Bruner, Jerome, (1960), *The Process of Education,* New York: Vintage Books, Random House.

Bruner, Jerome (1962), *On Knowing: Essays for the Left Hand,* Cambridge: Harvard University Press.

Bruner, Jerome, (1977), *A Study of Thinking,* New York: John Wiley.

Bruner, Jerome (1978), The Role of Dialogue in Language Acquisition, A. Sinclair, J. R. Jarviulle and W. J. M. Levett (Eds.), *The Child's Conception of Language,* New York: Springer-Verlag.

Campbell, Joseph (1988), *The Power of Myth,* New York: Doubleday.

Carbone, Peter F., Jr. (1991, summer), The Teacher as Philosopher, *The Educational Forum,* Vol. 55, Number 4.

Carnap, Rudolf (1931), The Old and the New Logic, *Logical Positivism,* (1959), A. J. Ayer (Ed.), New York: The Free Press.

Carnap, Rudolf, (1932), The Elimination of Metaphysics Through Logical Analysis, *Logical Positivism* (1959), A. J. Ayer, (Ed.), New York: The Free Press.

Caton, Charles E. (1970), (Ed.), *Philosophy and Ordinary Language,* Chicago: University of Illinois Press.

Charles, R., F. K. LesterJr. a nd P. O'Daffer (1987), *How to Evaluate Progress in Problem Solving,* Palo Alto: Dale Seymour Publications.

Chisholm, Roderick M. (1963), The Logic of Knowing, *Journal of Philosophy.*

Chisholm, Roderick M. (1966), *Theory of Knowledge,* Englewood Cliffs: Prentice-Hall, Inc.

Chomsky, Noam (1974), *Reflections on Language,* New York: Pantheon Books, Random House.

Chubb, John E. and Terry M. Moe (1990), *Politics, Markets & America's Schools,* Washington, D. C: The Brookings Institution.

Cohen, David K . (1984, February), "...the condition of teachers' work...," *Harvard Educational Review,* pp. 11-15.

Coleman, James S. (1961), *The Adolescent Society: The Social Life of the Teenager and its Impact on Education*, New York: Free Press.

Coleman, James S., Lee Rainwater and Kent McClelland (1978), *Social Standing in America*, New York: Basic Books, Inc.

Collingwood, R. G., (1956), *The Idea of History*, New York: Oxford University Press.

Collins, Peter (1970, February), Some Philosophical Reflections on Teaching and Learning, *The Teachers College Record*.

Cook, William J.(1988), *The Urgency of Change: The Metamorphosis of America's Schools*, Montgomery, Alabama: Underdog Press.

Cooper, John M. (1990), *Plato's Theatetus*, New York: Garland Publishing Company.

Copi, Irving M. (1982), *Introduction to Logic*, New York: Macmillan Publishing Company, Inc.

Cremin, Lawrence A. (Ed.) (1957), *The Republic and The School: Horace Mann On the Education of Free Men*, New York: Teachers College Press, Columbia University.

Cremin, Lawrence A., (1961), *The Transformation of the School: Progressivism in American Education*, 1876-1957, New York:

Cruse, Harold (1967), *The Crisis of the Negro Intellectual*, New York: William Morrow.

Danto, Arthur A. (1965), *Analytical Philosophy of History*, New York: Cambridge University Press.

DeAngelo, Edward (1970), Philosophers as Critical Thinking Consultants, *School and Society*, Vol. 98.

DeBono, E. (1970), *Lateral Thinking*, New York: Harper & Row.

Dewey, John (1916), *Democracy and Education*, New York: The Macmillan Company.

Dewey, John (1927), *The Public and Its Problems*, New York: Henry Holt and Company.

Dewey, John (1929), *The Quest for Certainty: A Study of the Relation of Knowledge* and Action, New York: G. P. Putnam's Sons.

Dewey, John (1933, 1960), *How We Think: A Restatement of the Relation of Reflective Thinking to the Educative Process*, Boston: D. C.Heath and Company.

Dewey, John (1938), *Logic: The Theory of Inquiry*, New York: Henry Holt and Company.

Dewey, John (1938), *Experience and Education*, New York: Collier Books, The Macmillan Company.

D'Souza, Dinesh (1991, March), Illiberal Education, *The Atlantic Monthly*.

Duckworth, Eleanor (1984, February), "...what teachers know: the best knowledge base...," *Harvard Educational Review*, pp. 15-20.

Dunham, William (1990), *Journey Through Genius: The Great Theorems of Mathematics*, New York: John Wiley & Sons, Inc.

Durant, Will (1933), *The Story of Philosophy: The Lives and Opinions of the Great Philosophers*, New York: Simon and Schuster.

Durant, Will and Ariel (1968), *The Lessons of History*, New York: Simon and Schuster.

Dworkin, Martin S. (Ed.) (1959), *Dewey on Education*, New York: Teachers College Press, Columbia Univesity.

Ehrenberg, Lyle and Sydelle and David Durfee (1979), *BASCIS Teaching/Learning Strategies*, Miami Beach, FL: Institute for Curriculum and Instruction.

Engle, S. Morris, (1980), *Analyzing Informal Fallacies*, Englewood Cliff ,NJ,Prentice-Hall.

Engle, S. Morris (1986), *With Good Reason*, New York: St. Martin's Press.

Ennis, Robert H. (1969), *Logic in Teaching*, Englewood Cliffs: PrenticeHall.

Eodice, Alexander R. (1990, spring), Dewey and Wittgenstein on the Idea of Certainty, *Philosophy Today*.

Ferre, Frederick (1987), *Language, Logic and God*, Chicago: University of Chicago Press.

Fischer, David Hackett (1970), *Historians' Fallacies*, New York: Harper & Row.

Habits of the Mind

Fitzgibbons, Robert (1981), *Making Educational Decisions: An Introduction to Philosophy*, New York: HBC.

Flew, Antony (1979), *A Dictionary of Philosophy*, New York: St. Martin's Press.

Gardiner, Patrick (1959), (Ed.), *Theories of History*, Glencoe, IL:The Free Press.

Geach, P. T. (1976), *Reason and Argument*, Berkley: University of California Press.

Goodlad, John I. (1976), *Facing the Future: Issues in Education and Schooling*, New York: McGraw-Hill Book Company.

Goodlad, John I. (1984), *A Place Called School*, New York: McGraw-Hill, Inc.

Goodlad, John I. (1990), *Teachers for our Nation's Schools*, San Francisco: S. F. Jossey-Bass.

Goodlad, John I., Roger Soder and Kenneth A. Sirotnik (Eds.) (1990), *The Moral Dimensions of Teaching*, San Francisco: S. F. Jossey Bass.

Goodlad, John I., Roger Soder and Kenneth A Sirotnik (Eds.) (1990), *Places Where Teachers are Taught,*, San Francisco: Jossey-Bass.

Gowin, D. B. (January 1963), Can Educational Theory Guide Practice? *Educational Theory*, pp. 6-12.

Grayling, A. C. (1982), *An Introduction to Philosophical Logic*, New York: Barnes & Noble Books, Inc.

Green, Thomas F. (1963, November), The Importance of Fairy Tales, *The Educational Forum*.

Green, Thomas F. (1971), *The Activities of Teaching*, New York: McGraw-Hill Book Company.

Grice, H. P. and P. F. Strawson, In Defense of a Dogma, in James F. Harris, Jr. and Richard H. Severence (Eds.), Chicago: *Analyticity*, Quadrangle Books.

Gross, Barry R. (1970), *Analytic Philosophy: An Historical Introduction*, New York: Pegasus Books.

Halverson, William H. (1967), *A Concise Introduction to Philosophy*, New York: Random House.

Harris, James F., Jr. and Richard H. Severence (Eds.), (1970), *Analyticity,* Chicago: Quadrangle Books.

Hegel, George Wilhelm Fredrich (1956), *The Philosophy of History,* New York: Dover Publications, Inc.

Heidegger, Martin (1968), *What Is Called Thinking?* New York: Perennial Library, Harper & Row, Publishers.

Heilbroner, Robert (1988, October), Is America Falling Behind?An Interview with Paul Kennedy, *American Heritage.*

Herzberg, F., B. Mausner and B. Snyderman (1959), *The Motivation to Work,* New York: John Wiley.

Hersh, Richard, H., (1983, May), How to Avoid Becoming a Nation of Technopeasants, *Phi Delta Kappan,* reprinted in *School Research Forum* (May 1983), pp. 57-63.

Hesiod 1959), *Works and Days, Theogeny,* Ann Arbor: University of Michigan Press.

Higginbotham, James (1992, February), Truth and Understanding, *Philosophical Studies,* pp. 3-16.

Honig, Bill (1990, February 28), 'Comprehensive Strategy' Can Improve Schools, *Education Week.*

Hoffer, Eric (1966), *The True Believer,* New York: Harper & Row, Perennial Library.

Hookway, Christopher (1992), *Peirce,* New York: Routledge & Kagan Paul.

Hospers, John (1967), *An Introduction to Philosophical Analysis,* Englewood Cliffs: Prentice-Hall.

Howe, Harold II (1984, February), Symposium on the Year of the Reports: Responses from the Educational Community, *Harvard Educational Review,* pp. 1-5.

Huizinga, Johan (1950), *Homo Ludens: A Study of t he Play-Element in Culture:* Boston: The Beacon Press.

Hullfish, H. Gordon and Philip G. Smith (1961), *Reflective Thinking: The Method of Education,* New York: Dodd, Mead and Company.

Hutchins, Robert M. (1953), *The Conflict i n Education in a Democratic Society,* New York: Harper & Row, Publishers.

Information Society (The): Are High School Graduates Ready? (1982, September), Denver, Colorado: Education Commission of the States.

James, William (1899), *Talks To Teachers On Psychology: And To Students on Some of Life's Ideals,* New York: Henry Holt and Company

Jencks, Christopher, et al (1972), Inequality: *A Reassessment of the Effect of Family and Schooling in America,* New York: Basic Books, Inc.

Jencks, Christopher, et al (1979), *Who Gets Ahead? The Determinants of Economic Success in America,* New York: Basic Books, Inc.

Johnson-Laird, P. N. (1983), *Mental Models: Towards A Cognitive Science of Language, Inference, and Consciousness,* Cambridge: Harvard University Press.

Jones, W. T. (1952), *History of Western Philosophy,* New York: Harcourt, Brace & World.

Jones, W. T. (1969), *Hobbes to Hume,* New York: Harcourt, Brace & Jovanovich.

Jones, W. T. (1969), *Kant to Wittgenstein and Sartre,* New York: Harcourt, Brace & Jovanovich.

Jones, W. T. (1975), *Kant and the Eighteenth Century,* New York: Harcourt, Brace & Jovanovich.

Jordan, Philip D. (1960, May), The Usefulness of Useless Knowledge, *The Historian.*

Jowett, Benjamin (Tr.) (1953), *The Dialogues of Plato,* Oxford: The Clarendon Press.

Kant, Immanuel (1929, 1965),*Critique of Pure Reason,* New York: St Martin's Press.

Kaplan, Abraham (1964), *The Conduct of Inquiry,* San Francisco: ChandlerPublishing Company.

Katz, Michael B. (1987), *Reconstructing American Education,* Cambridge: Harvard University Press.

Kearns, David T. and Denis P. Doyle (1988), *Winning The Brain Race: A Bold Plan to Make Our Schools Competitive,* San Francisco: Institute For Contemporary Studies.

Kennedy, Paul (1987), *The Rise and Fall of the Great Powers: Economic and Military Conflict From 1500 to 2000,* Vintage Books, Random House.

Kiernan, Thomas (1962) (Ed.), *Aristotle Dictionary,* New York: Philosophical Library.

Kimpston, Richard D., Howard Y. Williams and William S. Stockton (1992, winter), Ways of Knowing and the Curriculum, *The Educational Forum,* Vol. 50, No. 2, pp. 153-172.

Kneale, William and Martha (1978), *The Development of Logic,* Oxford: Clarendon Press.

Kohl, Herbert (1984, January), Who Are These Educational "Experts"...And What Are They Really Up To?, *Learning: The Magazine for Creative Teaching,*pp. 26-29.

Kroeber, A. L. (1944), *Configurations of Cultural Growth,* Los Angeles: University of California Press.

Krug, Edward A. (Ed.) (1961), *Charles W. Eliot and Popular Education,* New York: Teachers College Press, Columbia, University.

Kuhn, Thomas (1970), *The Structure of Scientific Revolutions,* Chicago: University of Chicago Press.

Kurfiss, Joanne G. (1988), *Critical Thinking: Theory, Research, Practice, and Possibilities,* Washington, D. C: The George Washington University Press.

Lacey, A. R. (1986), *A Dictionary of Philosophy,* London: Routledge & Kegan Paul.

Langer, Susan (1941, 1957), *Philosophy In A New Key: A Study in the Symbolism of Reason, Rite, and Art,* Cambridge: Harvard University Press.

Larrabee, Harold A. (1945), *Reliable Knowledge,* New York: HoughtonMifflin Company.

Lee, Gordon C. (Ed.) (1961), *Crusade Against Ignorance,* New York: Teachers College Press, Columbia University.

Lerner, Max (1957), *America As Civilization,* New York: Simon and Schuster.

Leonard, George (1992, May), The End of School, *The Atlantic Monthly,* pp. 24-32.

Lewis, Ann (1989), *Restructuring America's Schools,* Arlington, VA: American Association of School Administrators.

Lipman, Matthew, Ann Margaret Sharp and Frederick S. Oscanyan (1977), *Philosophy in the Classroom*, Upper Montclair, NJ: The Institute for The Advancement of Philosophy for Children.

Loomis, Louise R. (1942), (Ed.), *Plato*, New York: Classic Books.

Loomis, Louise R. (1943), (Ed.), *Aristotle: On Man In T he Universe*, New York: Classic Books.

MacIntyre, Alasdair (1984), *After Virtue*, 2nd ed., Notre Dame: University of Notre Dame Press.

MacKinnon, Edward (1985), *Basic Reasoning*, Englewood Cliffs: Prentice-Hall.

Marzano, *Robert J. et al (1988), Dimensions of Thinking: A Framework for Curriculum and Instruction*, Alexandria, VA: Association for Supervision and Curriculum Development.

Marzano, Robert J. (1990), Language, The Language Arts, and Thinking, *Handbook of Research on Teaching The English Language Arts*, New York: Macmillan Publishing Company.

Marzano, Robert J. (1991), *Dimensions of Learning: A New Paradigm for Curriculum, Instruction and Assessment*, Aurora, CO: Mid-Continent Regional Educational Laboratory.

Maritain, Jacques (1961), *On The Uses of Philosophy*, Westport, CT: Greenwood Press, Publishers.

Mates, Benson (1970), Synonymity, James F. Harris, Jr. and Richard H. Severence (Eds.), *Analyticity*, Chicago: Quadrangle Books.

McCall, Morgan W., Michael M. Lombardo and Ann M. Morrison (1988), (Eds.), *The Lessons of Experience*. Lexington, MA: Lexington Books, D. C. Heath and Company.

McKeon, Richard, (1941), (Ed.), *The Basic Works of Aristotle*, New York: Random House.

Mill, John Stuart (1973), *A System of Logic: Ratiocination and Induction, 2 vols.*, Toronto: University of Toronto Press, Routledge & Metheun.

Miller, Ed. L. (1995), *God and Reason: An Invitation to Philosophical Theology*, Englewood Cliffs, NJ: Prentice Hall.

Montagu, Ashley (1958), *Education and Human Relations*, Westport, CT: Greenwood Press, Publishers.

Morris, Van Cleve (1961), *Philosophy and the American School*, Boston: Houghton Mifflin Company.

Muller, Herbert J. (1957), *The Uses of the Past: Profiles of Former Societies*, New York: Oxford University Press.

Munson, Ronald (1976), *The Way of Words: An Informal Logic*, New York: Houghton Mifflin Company.

Nash, Paul (1966), *Authority and Freedom in Education: An Introduction to the Philosophy of Education*, New York: John Wiley and Sons, Inc.

National Tests: What Other Countries Expect Their Students to Know (1991), Washington, D. C., National Endowment for the Humanities.

Newell, R. W. (1967), *The Concept of Philosophy*, London: Methuen & Co., Ltd.

Newman, John Cardinal(1886), *The Idea of a University*, London Longman, Green & Company.

Ogden, C. K. and I. A. Richards (1923), *The Meaning of Meaning*, New York: Harcourt, Brace & World, Inc.

Oliver, Donald (1990, September), Grounded Knowing: A PostmodernPerspective on Teaching and Learning, *Educational Leadership*.

O'Neil, John (1992, March), On Education and the Economy: A Conversation with Marc Tucker, *Educational Leadership*.

Passow, A. Harry (1984, June), Tackling the Reform Reports of the 1980s, *Phi Delta Kappan*, pp. 674-683.

Paul, Richard, A. J. A. Binker and Marla Charbonneau (1986), *Critical Thinking Handbook: K-3: A Guide for Remodelling Lesson Plans in Language Arts, Social Studies and Science*, Robnert Part, CA: Center for Critical Thinking and Moral Critique.

Paul, Richard, A. J. A. Binker, Douglas Martin and Ken Adamson (1986), *Critical Thinking Handbook: High School: A Guide for Redesigning Instruction*, Robnert Part, CA: Center for Critical Thinking and Moral Critique.

Peters, R. S. (1967), *Ethics and Education*, Glenview, IL: Scott, Foresman & Company.

Peters, Thomas J. and Robert H. Waterman, Jr.(1982), *In Search of Excellence: Lessons from America's Best-Run Companies*, New York: Harper & Row, Publishers.

Phenix, Philip H. (1964), *Realms of Meaning,* New York: McGraw-Hill Book Company.

Plato, *Timaeus and Critias* (1977), translated by Desmond Lee, New York: Penguin Books.

Polanyi, Michael (1967), *The Tacit Dimension*, New York: Anchor Books.

Popper, Karl (1957), *The Poverty of Historicism*, London: Routledge & Kegan Paul.

Pratte, Richard (1973), *The Public School Movement: A Critical Study,* New York: McKay.

Pratte, Richard (1988), *Civil Imperative: Examining the Need for Civic Education,* New York: Teachers College Press.

Pratte, Richard (1992), *Philosophy ofEducation,* Springfield, Il: Charles Thomas.

Peursen, C. A. Van (1970), *Ludwig Wittgenstein: AnIntroduction to His Philosophy,* New York: E. P. Dutton.

Pusch, James (1992, winter), Metaphor and Teaching, *The Educational Forum*, Vol. 56, No. 2, pp. 185-192.

Quine, Willard Van Orman (1971), *From a Logical Point of View,* Cambridge, Mass: Harvard University Press.

Quine, Willard Van Orman (1980), *Elementary Logic,* Cambridge: Harvard University Press.

Randall, John Herman Jr. (1960), *Aristotle,* New York: Columbia University Press.

Rauch, Jonathan (1989, August), Kids As Capital, *The Atlantic Monthly.*

Ravitch, Diane (1983), *The Troubled Decade: American Education, 1945-1980,* New York: Vintage Books.

Reagan, Gerald M. (1982, summer), Constraints on Academic Freedom, *The Educational Forum*, pp. 391-402.

Reese, William L. (1980), *Dictionary of Philosophy and Religion,* New Jersey: Humanities Press.

Reichenbach, Hans (1970), *Experience and Prediction,* Chicago: The University of Chicago Press.

Rhodes, Lewis A. (1992, March), On the Road to Quality, *Educational Leadership,* pp. 76-80.

Rokeach, Milton (1960), *The Open and Closed Mind,* New York: Basic Books, Inc.

Rosenberg, Jay F. (1978), *The Practice of Philosophy: A Handbook for Beginners,* Englewood Cliffs: Prentice-Hall, Inc.

Rugg, Harold (1947), *Foundations for American Education,* New York: World Book Company.

Russell, Bertrand (1905, October), On Denoting, in Douglas Lackey (Ed.), *Essays in Analysis: Bertrand Russell,* New York: George Braziller, Inc.

Ryle, Gilbert (1949), *The Concept of Mind,* New York:Barnes & Noble.

Salmon, Wesley C. (1963), *Logic,* Englewood Cliffs: Prentice-Hall.

Scheffler, Israel (1965), *The Conditions of Knowledge,* Chicago: Scott, Foresman.

Scheffler, Israel (1974), *The Language of Education,* Springfield, IL: Charles C. Thomas, Publisher.

Schlick, Moritz (1931), The Turning Point in Philosophy, *Logical Positivism* (1959), A. J. Ayer, Ed., New York: The Free Press.

Schlick, Moritz, (1934),The Foundation of Knowledge, *Logical Positivism* (1959), A. J. Ayer (Ed., New York: The Free Press.

Schmitt, Bernadotte E. (1961, January), With How Little Wisdom, *American Historical Review.*

Schwab, Joseph,(1962, July), The Concept of the Structure of Discipline,*The Educational Record,* Vol. 43.

Schwab, Joseph (1964), Problems, Topics and Issues, *Education and the Structure of Knowledge,* Stanley Elam (Ed.), Chicago: Rand McNally and Company.

Schwab, J oseph (1964), Structure of the Disciplines: Meaning and Significance, *The Structure of Knowledge and the Curriculum,* G. W. Ford and Lawrence Pugno (Eds.), Chicago: Rand McNally and Company.

Schwab, Joseph (November 1968),The Practical: A Language for Curriculum, *School Review,* pp. 1-23.

Schwab, Joseph (August 1971), The Practical: Arts of Eclectic, *School Review,* pp. 493-542.

Sewell, G. T. (1982, May), Against Anomie and Amnesia: What Basic Education Means in the Eighties, *Phi Delta Kappan,* pp. 603-606.

Singal, Daniel J. (1991, November), The Other Crisis in American Education, *The Atlantic Monthly.*

Smith, B. Othanel and Robert H. Ennis (1961), *Language and Concepts in Education,* Chicago: Rand McNally and Company.

Smith, Page, *Killing The Spirit* (1990), New York: Viking Press.

Snow, C. P. (1965), *The Two Cultures: And A Second Look*, New York: The Cambridge University Press.

Soames, Scott (1992, February), Truth, Meaning , and Understanding, *Philosophical Studies*, pp. 17-35.

Soltis, Jonas F. (1968), *An Introduction to the Analysis of Educational Concepts*, Reading, MA: Addison-Wesley Publishing Company.

Soltis, J onas F. (Ed.) (1981) *Philosophy and Education, Eightieth Yearbook of the National Society for the Study of Education,* Part I, Chicago: University of Chicago Press.

Stiles, John (1992, March), The Unstudious American: Who's at Fault?, *Educational Leadership, pp. 61-63.*

Stout, Jeffrey (1986, spring & summer), Liberal Society and the Language of Morals, *Soundings: An Interdisciplinary Journal,* pp. 32-59.

Strauss, Leo and Joseph Cropsey (Eds.) (1972), History of Political Philosophy, Chicago: University of Chicago Press.

Sternberg, R obert J. (1986, October), Synthesis of Research on the Effectiveness of Intellectual Skills Programs: Snake Oil Remedies or Miracle Cures? *Educational Leadership*, pp. 60-68.

Sternberg, Robert J. (1986), *Intelligence Applied: Understanding and Increasing Your Intellectual Skills,* San Diego: Harcourt, Brace and Jovanovich.

Sternberg, Robert J. (1991, April), Creating Creative Minds, *Phi Delta Kappan.*

Stone, I. F. (1988), *The Trial of Socrates,* New York: Doubleday Books.

Stout, Jeffrey (1986, spring/summer), Liberal Society And The Language of Morals, *Soundings: An Interdisciplinary Journal,* pp. 32-59.

Strawson, P. F. (1974), *Subject and Predicate in Logic and Grammar,* London: Methuen & Company, Ltd.

Swain, Joseph Ward (1950), *The Ancient World,* Vol. One, New York: Harper & Brothers.

Tarnas, Richard (1991), *The Passion of the Western Mind: Understanding the Ideas that Have Shaped Our World View,* New York: Ballentine Books.

Timar, Thomas and David L.Kirp (March 1989), Education Reform in the 1980's: Lessons from the States, *Phi Delta Kappan,* pp. 509-10.

Thomas, Stephen N. (1977), *Practical Reasoning In Natural Language,* Englewood Cliffs: Prentice-Hall, Inc.

Thompson, Loren J. (1973, February), History, Historians and Logic, *Theory Into Practice.*

Thompson, Loren J. (1975, May), The Nature and Need of Theory, *The Educational Forum.*

Tice, Terrence N. and Thomas P. Slavens (1983), *Research Guide to Philosophy,* Chicago: American Library Association.

Toch, Thomas (1991) *I n The Name of Excellence: The Struggle to Reform the Nation's Schools, Why It's Failing and What Should be Done,* New York: Oxford University Press.

Toulmin, Stephen, Richard Rieke and Allan Janik (1984),*An Introduction to Reasoning,* New York: Macmillan Publishing Company, Inc.

Twain, Mark (1965), *The Adventures of Huckleberry Finn,* New York: Harper Classics, Harper & Row, Publishers.

Vivian, Frederick (1969), *Thinking Philosophically: An introduction for Students,* New York: Basic Books, Inc.

Walton, Susan (1983, August 31), "There Has Been a Conspiracy of Silence About Teaching: B. F. Skinner Argues That Pedagogy Is Key to School Reforms, *Education Week.*

Wellman, Robert R. (1965, summer), Cicero: Education for Humanitas, *Harvard Educational Review.*

Whimbey, Arthur and Jack Lockhead (1986), *Problem Solving and Comprehension*, Hillsdale, NJ: Lawrence Erlbaum Associates, Publishers.

White, Morton (1965), *Foundations of Historical Knowledge*, New York: Harper and Row.

Whitehead, Alfred North (1929), *The Function of Reason*, Boston: Beacon Press.

Whitehead, Alfred North (1929), *The Aims of Education and Other Essays*, New York: The Macmillan Company.

Whitehead, Alfred North (1936, September), Harvard: The Future, *The Atlantic Monthly.*

Whitehead, Alfred North (1933), *Adventures in Ideas*, New York: The Macmillan Company.

Whorf, B. L. (1956), *Language, Thought and Reality*, Cambridge: Massachusetts Institute of Technology Press.

Wilshire, Bruce(1990), *The Moral Collapse of the University: Professionalism, Purity and Alienation*, Albany: State University of New York Press.

Wilson, John (1966), *Thinking With Concepts*, Cambridge: The University Press.

Wittgenstein, Ludwig (1951), *Tractatus Logico-Philosophicus*, New York: Humanities Press.

Wittgenstein, Ludwig (1958), *Philosophical Investigations*, New York: The Macmillan Company.

Wright, Robert (1991, April), Quest for the Mother Tongue, *The Atlantic Monthly.*

Wyatt, Carolyn D. (1984, February) "...a missing and essential element...," Harvard Educational Review, pp. 28-31.

Yost, Avila M. and E. B. Wexler (1977), Effects of Learning of Post-Instructional Responses To Questions of Differing Degrees of Complexity, *Journal of Educational Psychology.*

Zuboff, S. (1988), *In the Age of the Smart Machine*, New York: Basic Books, Inc.

Index

Author's Biographical Sketch

Following service in the United States Navy during the Korean War, Loren Thompson earned a masters degree in history from the University of Delaware. He then spent 30 years in education, as a teacher and administrator and as a university teacher. During this time, he earned a Ph.D. at The Ohio State University. He and his wife now live in Colorado. This is his first book.